SECRET GILLINGHAM

Philip MacDougall

AMBERLEY

First published 2019

Amberley Publishing
The Hill, Stroud
Gloucestershire, GL5 4EP

www.amberley-books.com

Copyright © Philip MacDougall, 2019

The right of Philip MacDougall to be identified as the
Author of this work has been asserted in accordance
with the Copyrights, Designs and Patents Act 1988.

ISBN 978 1 4456 8925 8 (print)
ISBN 978 1 4456 8926 5 (ebook)

British Library Cataloguing in Publication Data.
A catalogue record for this book is available from the
British Library.

Origination by Amberley Publishing.
Printed in Great Britain.

Contents

Introduction

Secret Gillingham is a companion volume to my two earlier books in this series, *Secret Chatham* and *Secret Rochester*. It looks at Gillingham in previous times, concentrating on lesser-known aspects of its history, or delving a little further into affairs that are long forgotten. While the Dutch raid on Chatham during the summer of 1667 is generally well known, much less written about is the massive battle fought off Gillingham and the later defences built round Gillingham to prevent a future enemy conducting a similar attack. Also included is an account of Gillingham's hidden population: the prisoners of war who lived offshore within the parish of Gillingham for many decades but were not included in the census count of 1801. They lived in quite appalling conditions, with many of the other inhabitants of Gillingham not even knowing of their existence. A much happier period in Gillingham's history was an attempt to create a seaside resort to rival Margate, with the fashionable of London descending on a section of beach lying close to the present-day Strand. It didn't last long, but for a short period of time those behind the scheme were certainly coining it in. Little known, and reserved for the last chapter, is the utterly bewildering failure of the borough council, back in the 1930s, to adequately prepare the town for a war that everybody knew was heading this way, with every chance that Gillingham, with its dockyard, would be on the front line. At one time, the government even attempted to step in, telling the local authority that air-raid shelters were needed and even more needed was the recruitment of adequate numbers for the various branches of civil defence.

1. The Will Adams Connection

When Gillingham-born Will Adams landed on the shores of Japan in April 1600, he was unsure of the reception he would receive. The pilot-major of a Dutch squadron of five trading ships that had set out from Holland for the East Indies eighteen months earlier, he was stepping into enemy territory. The Portuguese, inveterate opponents of all Protestants and the countries they came from, were already trading with the Japanese and would not tolerate interlopers. Would they convince the nation's rulers that Will Adams and the Dutchmen accompanying him were best suited to a prison cell or a hangman's noose? For the crews of those five ships that had originally set out, nothing had gone easy. Passing into the Pacific by way of the Straits of Magellan, three were wrecked in storms and another forced to return home. As for that one remaining ship, *Liefde*, which Adams was aboard, this barely made landfall on the coast of Japan. Only five of its crew were able to walk ashore, the rest were too weak and debilitated to leave the vessel unaided.

Will Adams as he is presumed to have appeared in 1598, the year in which he set out on a trading expedition that would bring him to the coast of Japan where he was shipwrecked. As the holder of a Trinity House licence he had been appointed pilot-major of a Dutch expedition, the object of which was to establish trading links with various Far East nations.

The particular ship given over to Will Adams was *Liefde*, the only ship to reach Japan. The other ships of the expedition were either lost at sea or forced to make a judicious return to Europe. Even *Liefde* only just made it to Japan, with her few remaining crew members victims of disease and close to starvation.

Upon learning of the arrival of these foreigners, Portuguese Jesuit priests accompanying the merchants of their country were soon spreading the message that Adams and his fellow crew members should be hanged, declaring them to be 'pestilent fellows' guilty of piracy. This might have been the end of Will Adams and his mercantile expedition if it had not been for the intervention of Tokugawa Ieyasu – the military ruler of Japan and founder of the Tokugawa Shōgunate. He was especially interested in acquiring the cannons and gunpowder that the vessel had been carrying for its own defence. Tokugawa demanded that Adams, as the most senior of the surviving crew, be brought to his palace at Edo (the former name of Tokyo) where he, personally, could interrogate him. On hearing what Adams had to say for himself, Tokugawa finally brought the meeting to an end with a single word – a word that Adams did not understand. Immediately whisked away and placed under close confinement, Adams was, nevertheless, treated well, but with his fate seemingly in the balance. Finally, after six weeks, he was put out of his misery and was called again to appear before Tokugawa where he was informed that he was to advise on all matters to do with the sea and overseas trade and also share his knowledge of western seafaring practices.

Adams was to become a man of great importance in Japan, something denied to him in England. The downside was that Tokugawa considered him to be so important that he was never allowed to return to England; Adams never saw his English wife and two children again. Although a seafarer rather than a shipwright, Tokugawa commanded

Adams to build him two ships, which were to be in the European style and capable of long-distance voyaging. At that time, vessels available to the Japanese were lightweight and quite incapable of long voyages. Setting himself to the new task, Adams was to oversee the construction of two vessels – one of 80 tons and the second of 120 tons. Both were built in the harbour of Itō. Adams taught carpenters from the harbour the skills of selecting the right timbers and the methods used in the West for cutting, shaping and fitting them into place. Through being the first large ships built in Japan and entering into the service of the shōgun, Adams is sometimes credited with being the founder of the Japanese navy – his story was told to Japanese children for many centuries. A monument at Itō, overlooking the harbour, was erected to mark his achievement of being the first Englishman to set foot on Japanese soil.

Unlike Adams, much more certain of their reception were the highly skilled crews of two Japanese warships that arrived in Gillingham in June 1907. While not the first of the Japanese nation to set foot in England, they represented the first tangible evidence of a grand alliance that, by then, existed between Japan and Great Britain. Signed in 1902, it was a defensive treaty designed to prevent Russian expansion to the east, with the alliance offering clear-cut advantages to both countries. For Britain it permitted naval economies through allowing a reduction of warships that would otherwise need to be placed on the Far East station. For the Japanese it allowed this rapidly expanding military nation the opportunity to acquire direct experience of British naval practice.

By then Japan was already a force with which to be reckoned. Over the last forty years she had undergone a naval transformation that had seen a tiny sail-powered fleet totally replaced by a large force of coal-powered battleships and cruisers. In fact, by then, Japan was considered to have reached parity with a number of western nations, including France and the USA.

To begin with, this expansion had been achieved through the purchase of ready-made hulls from British shipyards. To these, sophisticated shell-firing guns were added, which were normally ordered from Krupp in Germany. This, of course, had been an essential first stage in the development of a modern navy, and these purchases were used as a model upon which the Japanese shipyards could base their own designs in future years.

This Anglo-Japanese alliance was to last for approximately twenty years. During those early years it became customary for the ships of one nation to visit the ports of the other. An important activity for bonding the alliance, it also ensured that the public in both countries were aware that such an alliance existed. It was for this reason that the important dockyard town of Gillingham was to play host to those two Japanese warships, with a further visit occurring in 1910.

The two ships that came in 1907 were *Tsukuba* and *Chitose*. Both were berthed in Basin 3 at the Gillingham end of the dockyard and entered through the Bull's Nose, close to Gillingham Pier. The two vessels were immediately the subject of great curiosity, not just because of their crews having come from the mythical East, but through *Chitose*, a 4,760-ton cruiser, having proven herself in battle at the Japanese victory over the Russian fleet at Tsu-Shima, fought just two years earlier. *Tsukuba*, on the other hand, was an entirely new design, completed a few months earlier at the Kure yard. An armoured cruiser of 13,750 tons with an incredible speed of 24 knots, she was the first major capital ship to be

The dockyard at the time of the Japanese naval visits. Although usually referred to as Chatham dockyard, much of the dockyard lay within Gillingham.

Looking across Basin 2 towards Basin 3 where the visiting Japanese warships were berthed.

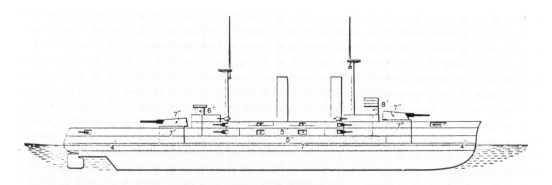

A profile drawing showing the general plan of the two sister ships *Ikoma* and *Tsukuba*, with the strength of armoured areas marked in inches. *Tsukuba* came to the Gillingham end of the dockyard in 1907 and *Ikoma* in 1910.

designed and constructed entirely in Japan. And, through carrying a main armament of four 12-inch guns and a secondary battery of twelve 6-inch guns, she was one of the most heavily armed cruisers of the day. Not surprisingly, both dockyard mateys and senior naval officials were striving to get a close-up view of this truly phenomenal warship.

Having berthed in Basin 3, the crew of the two Japanese ships were provided with a full programme of entertainment covering the eleven days in which the ships remained in the dockyard. Included were numerous garden parties, dinners for officers, ratings and petty officers at HMS *Pembroke* naval barracks and a visit to the Olympia horse show in London. An additional part of the agenda was a tour of mid-Kent, with Admiral Ijuin and twenty of his most senior officers conveyed around the countryside in a fleet of cars. The itinerary included Aylesford, Seal, Sevenoaks (for lunch at the Royal Crown Hotel), Knowle Park (to meet Lord Sackville) and Wrotham. A final stopping point was Cobham Hall where the party was welcomed by the Countess of Darnley and given tea.

Undoubtedly, the major event of the two ships arriving in Gillingham took place on Wednesday 12 June when the mayors of the three towns each organised a civic reception – in those days Chatham, Gillingham and Rochester rarely worked together. The first of these receptions was in Gillingham, with 250 immaculately dressed petty officers and ratings conveyed by six trams to Gillingham Park. Those on the open-top decks would have got a fine view of the crowded ranks of shops and homes as they passed through the High Street and along Canterbury Street – even in those days this was very much a hallmark of Gillingham. Many were occupied by those employed in the dockyard and, to mark the occasion, most were lavishly decorated with British and Japanese flags. Nothing less could be expected from a population proud of its dockyard heritage, highly welcoming to any allied visiting navy.

On disembarking from the trams and entering Gillingham Park, tea and cakes were freely available with the mayor, Alderman R. Edwards, giving a carefully prepared speech in which, quite predictably, he made reference to Will Adams who he referred to as 'the Englishman who was also the pioneer of the Japanese Imperial Navy'. He went on to add that 'Gillingham must have a peculiar fascination for the Japanese, as it was a Gillingham

Trams were the means by which 250 immaculately dressed Japanese naval petty officers and ratings were conveyed to Gillingham Park where they were entertained with an address given by the Mayor of Gillingham.

Gillingham Park, seen here in 1934. It was here, shortly after the Anglo-Japanese naval alliance was signed, that sailors of the Japanese Imperial Navy were regaled by the Mayor of Gillingham.

The entrance gate to Gillingham Park, through which the 250 naval ratings would have passed.

man who was the first Englishman to put his foot on the shores of Japan', referring, of course, to Will Adams.

It is recorded that the Japanese seamen to whom the mayor spoke were all familiar with the name of Adams and seemed most appreciative when his name was mentioned. Shortly after, the trams were reboarded, this time bound for Chatham where, of all things, they were offered lunch in the form of Indian kedgeree. Apparently the organisers were not fully acquainted with the origin of certain Far Eastern delicacies, believing that kedgeree, through being an Asian dish, would suffice. A *Chatham News* reporter, while describing the meal as 'good', did not quite think it the done thing. In Rochester a substantial tea, without kedgeree, was provided at the Guildhall following a tour of the city's historic sites.

That second Japanese naval visit took place in July 1910, coinciding with a Japan-British exhibition at White City in London. On this occasion, the visiting warship was *Ikoma*, sister-ship of *Tsukuba* then undertaking her commissioning voyage. She also berthed in Basin 3, with 420 of her crew visiting the exhibition in White City. Arriving on the 27th of that month, she remained there for the next six days before sailing to Portsmouth and then Devonport for a series of further receptions. As on the previous visit, receptions were organised in each of the Medway Towns, while a country picnic was organised by warrant officers of Pembroke naval barracks for the warrant officers of *Ikoma*. For *Ikoma*'s medical surgeons a tour of the recently opened Royal Naval Hospital, now Medway Maritime, was arranged.

Will Adams was born in Gillingham and baptised at St Mary's Church on 24 September 1564. The church itself has undergone some changes, but much of it still has the appearance that Adams would have known. It is not recorded whether any members of the Japanese crew visited the church. It is seen here at around the time of those two visits to Gillingham by Japanese warships. The church font, dating to the twelfth century and to be seen on the right, would have been used to baptise baby Will Adams.

'The Church on the Green'. A more recent view of St Mary Magdalene, the parish church where Will Adams was baptised.

Some national newspapers appear to have forgotten the earlier visit by *Tsukuba* and *Chitose*, describing this as the first visit to Great Britain by a Japanese warship, but were certainly correct when the readers of those same newspapers were informed that while a cruiser, *Tsukuba* carried heavier armour than thirty-nine of fifty-six British battleships. A few years later, both *Tsukuba* and *Ikoma* were more correctly redesignated as battle cruisers rather than armoured cruisers, which more correctly reflected their weight of armament and speed when at sea. It might be further added that these two cruisers were ahead of their time as similar ships for the Royal Navy only entered service in 1908 – one year after *Tsukuba*.

Despite a dramatic decline in the relationship of Britain and Japan following the ending of the First World War, then known only as the Great War, this did not prevent the two countries continuing to honour Will Adams as creator of the Japanese Imperial Navy. During a visit to Japan in 1925, a certain Major W. W. Grantham came across a memorial to Adams that overlooked the naval arsenal Yokosuka, one of Japan's principal shipyards, determining that a similar memorial should be erected in Kent, with Gillingham the obvious location. From this germ of an idea emerged – once Grantham had returned to England and taken up an appointment in Deal as a courtroom official – a campaign to raise money for the building of a memorial. This memorial, which was officially unveiled

On the second Japanese naval visit to Gillingham surgeons were invited to make an inspectional tour of the new naval hospital in Gillingham, as opened by Edward VII in July 1905. The building ceased being a naval hospital during the early 1960s when it was handed over to the NHS.

on 11 May 1934, once again brought a Japanese naval presence to the town, but in numbers somewhat less than those two earlier naval visits. After all, relations between Britain and Japan were now in decline. Instead of an entire warship, Gillingham witnessed only the arrival of a Japanese admiral – Vice-Admiral Hajime Matsushita, commander-in-chief of the Training Fleet. At that time, the training squadron he commanded, composed of two armoured cruisers, *Iwate* and *Asama*, was at Marseilles, with Matsushita travelling overland for the ceremony. He was also joined by the Japanese ambassador to Great Britain, Tsuneo Matsudaira.

Today, the Clock Tower memorial, still stands with a brass plaque in its original position alongside Watling Street. The plaque briefly records the various achievements of Will Adams, mentioning his work of constructing two vessels of European design and instructing 'his adopted countrymen' in gunnery, geography and mathematics while also referring to the memorial that Grantham had seen at Yokosuka.

The story of Will Adams, which also included his involvement in Japanese military affairs, was celebrated in Gillingham through the erection of this memorial clock tower, which was unveiled in 1934 and seen here in this more recent photo.

DID YOU KNOW?
Before Will Adams died in 1620, he left an injunction that, translated from Japanese, read, 'Having in my wanderings come to this land, I have until now lived in comfort and plenty, thanks entirely to the favour of the Tokugawa Shōgun. Be so good as to bury me on the summit of the Hemmi Hill, making my grave face to the east, so that I may behold Edo [Tokyo]. My soul being in the underworld shall ever have in protection this capital city.'

HAIL ! GILLINGHAM'S HERO

To coincide with the original unveiling of the Will Adams memorial one local newspaper, the *Chatham Observer*, produced a special booklet that it proceeded to advertise in the manner depicted.

TO-DAY the Japanese Ambassador unveils the memorial to WILL ADAMS. Read the story of Will's life and adventure in Japan. It is of great interest to all Medway folk.

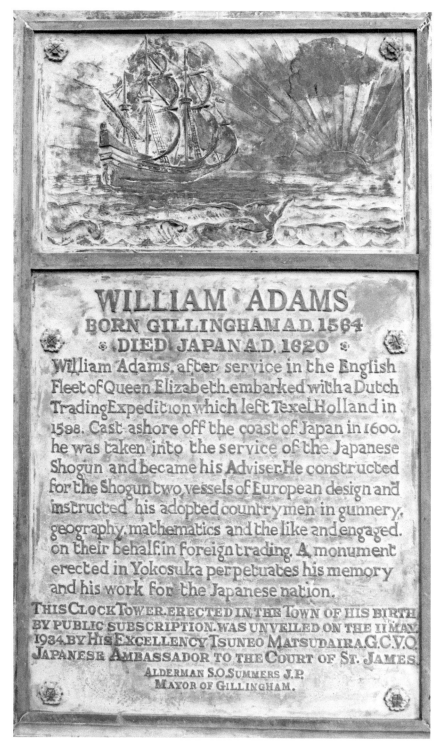

A brass plate attached to the memorial clock tower briefly outlines the life and achievements of Will Adams.

Order Date:	28/11/2019		
Customer Reference:	24851578 0015033182		
Despatch Note:	20191136510401		
Order Number:	1351988		

ISBN	Title	Qty	Returns Reason
9781445689258	Secret Gillingham	1	

20191136510401

2. Front-line Village

In Gillingham on Tuesday 11 June 1667, the question most local inhabitants must have been asking was should they stay or leave? A few days earlier, on the Saturday, an enemy squadron of Dutch warships had landed soldiers on both the Isle of Grain and the Isle of Sheppey at the mouth of the Medway. On the former they had battered down the church door and stolen the silver communion cup and other valuables. Those on Sheppey had set about destroying the dockyard at Sheerness and its defending fortress – both under construction at the time and ripe for the taking.

It didn't take a genius to conclude that Gillingham would be the next target for the attacking Dutch squadron, which was intent upon reaching Chatham for the purpose of destroying the country's most important naval dockyard. It was also clear that when the Dutch did reach Gillingham, by way of Long Reach, Pinup Reach and finally Gillingham Reach, there was going to be one almighty battle in which those on shore and those on board ships in the river would be confronting the possibility of horrendous injury or an agonising death. In the event, the simple surrendering of those sent to prevent the Dutch passing beyond Gillingham somewhat reduced the level of bloodshed; however, many from Gillingham, mostly women and children, did seek shelter elsewhere, unwilling to be caught up in such a deplorable affair.

Since May 1665 the Dutch had been at war with England and a number of battles between the fleets of the two countries were fought in the North Sea. For the Dutch, a knockout blow was required, something that would not only weaken the English navy, but cause such embarrassment that England would attempt to gain peace on any terms. For this, the destruction of Chatham dockyard, through both a nearby landing of troops and bombardment from the river, would hopefully result in such an outcome. Yet, it was a high-risk strategy. The Medway was no easy river to navigate, while there was always the possibility that adverse winds would trap the Dutch ships, allowing an English fleet to come into the river behind them, destroying their attacking squadron even before the task of destroying the dockyard had begun. To provide the Dutch with at least a fighting chance, a number of English seamen were recruited onto their ships who had a knowledge of the river and who could pilot the Dutch ships through the navigable channels while avoiding several highly treacherous sandbanks. Perhaps, also, God was on the side of the Dutch, or at least this was their claim, for the winds they needed to safely progress along the Medway and later return fortuitously remained in their favour.

Gillingham, then a small riverside village whose inhabitants were more or less equally dependent on fishing the rich waters of the Medway and farming the luscious expansive surrounding fields best suited to the growing of wheat and barley. Admittedly, a few villagers also worked in the dockyard, for while it then lay entirely within the boundaries of Chatham, it also lay within easy walking distance. Those worried and anxious villagers who hastily left the area were replaced by the equally urgent movement of soldiers brought into the area to face off the Dutch. Mostly they were Scots, men of a regiment commanded by Lord George Douglas and later taking the name Royal Scots. With them they brought a number of cannons, which were formed into batteries where fishermen had once repaired their nets.

To be defended at this point of the river were two ends of an iron chain that stretched across the river, which, once raised, served as a navigational barrier or boom defence that would supposedly deny access beyond Gillingham to the attacking Dutch ships. Extending from the Gillingham foreshore, where it could be raised and lowered by a windlass, it stretched across the river to Hoo Ness, a marshy island on the far side. In weight, the chain was in excess of 14 tons, with each of the iron links having a circumference of just over 6 inches. While no ship could possibly break the chain, its sheer weight was a problem: while supported by four floating stages at an equal distance apart, the chain at some points sagged to a depth of 9 feet.

In addition to soldiers and the rapid erection of gun batteries, a number of block ships, including some fairly large battleships, were brought to Gillingham Reach. These were placed on the up-water side of the chain, with their broadside guns facing towards the approaching Dutch squadron. Lacking crews, for these ships were out of commission, a few of Lord Douglas' men joined these vessels.

Essential for the defenders now mustering around the village of Gillingham was the advanced intelligence on the progress of the Dutch as they moved upriver. To this end, several light and fast small vessels, known as fly boats, were sent forward to bring back what information they could. Just as useful was the tower of St Mary's Church in Gillingham. From the top it was possible to gain a view along the full length of both Pinup and Long reaches – the two stretches of water along which the Dutch would need to proceed before reaching the chain. Almost certainly, officers from Lord Douglas' regiment would have taken up position in the tower, relaying to their troops all that they could see. Two weeks later, once the hurly-burly was done and the battle lost and won, the diarist John Evelyn sketched the river and the scene of several sunken ships, probably climbing to the top of the church tower for this purpose.

It was early on the morning of Wednesday 12 June that the Dutch squadron entered Gillingham Reach, their warships brought to a standstill by heavy cannon fire from both the gun battery on the Gillingham foreshore and the several block ships positioned either side of the chain. If the chain could be broken in some way, then the squadron could quickly pass this barrage, but if the chain proved impenetrable then the Dutch would be smashed to pieces, trapped by the chain and forced to make a slow retreat against the wind that was then blowing. To resolve the problem, Captain Jan van Brakel, commander of the *Vrede*, a fourth-rate warship, volunteered to take his vessel forward to engage one of the more powerful blockships on the near side of the chain, successfully bringing it under fire. The crew, formed of untrained watermen, were unsurprisingly quick to surrender. In so doing, this allowed two of the Dutch fireships to ram the chain, successfully riding over it and forcing the chain away from one of its supporting stages.

Gillingham Church tower was probably used by defenders at the time of the Dutch raid to get a full appreciation of what was happening on the river and where exactly the Dutch forces were at any particular time.

It was here, in this part of the river immediately off Gillingham, that much of the fighting between the English and Dutch took place.

The view from Upnor Castle looking across the Medway towards St Mary's Island. It was here, while still off Gillingham, that the Dutch were finally halted.

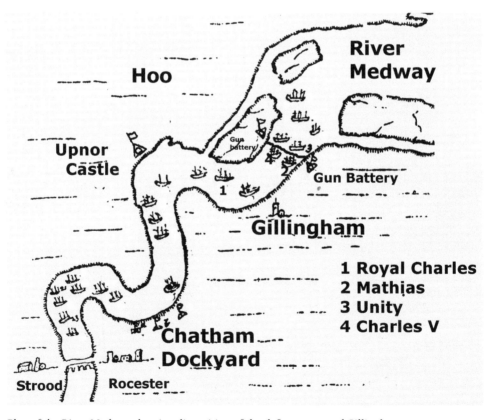

Plan of the River Medway showing disposition of the defences around Gillingham.

Upnor Castle during a more peaceful period of its existence and viewed along Upnor Reach, with the ships in the foreground moored off the tip of St Mary's Island.

Upnor Castle as seen from the Gillingham side of the river.

This was the moment the Dutch had been waiting for. Beyond the chain there were rich pickings: not only did Chatham dockyard lay ahead, but so did a number of warships that had been brought above the chain to protect them from the Dutch. All of them had but only a few men on board to man their guns, with three particularly prized ships – *Mathias* and *Charles V* soon captured and destroyed, and another great ship, *Royal Charles*, captured and eventually taken back to the Netherlands.

Once the waters around Gillingham were secured, troops were landed ashore, clearing it of any remaining defenders and capturing the hastily formed gun battery. While some looting had been witnessed on Grain and Sheppey, on this occasion strict orders had been issued by the Dutch that any of their soldiers caught looting or attacking civilians would be severely punished. Samuel Pepys, a senior naval official, remarked upon this after visiting Gillingham at the end of June:

> It seems remarkable to me, and of great honour to the Dutch, that those of them that did go on shore to Gillingham, though they went in fear of their lives, and were some of them killed ... yet killed none of our people nor plundered their houses, but did take things of easy carriage and left the rest, and not a house burned...

Although Pepys felt forced to add that Lord Douglas's men, upon them later returning to Gillingham after the Dutch had retreated, 'plundered and took all away' and that those living in and around Gillingham considered 'our own soldiers' to be far more 'terrible'.

The lesson of the Dutch raid was that the defences of the Medway had to be considerably strengthened, with the area around Gillingham, where a new chain was positioned shortly after the raid, needing to be surrounded by permanently positioned gun batteries. The man placed in charge of designing these defences was Bernard de Gomme (1620–83), a military engineer of Flemish descent who had already begun a programme of renewing fortifications in England, with the Dutch raid placing a new emphasis on him designing fortifications against a replicated Dutch-style raid.

Gillingham fort, built after the Dutch raid, was positioned close to the entrance of St Mary's Creek. As constructed, it was a square redoubt, 11 metres (36 feet) in height and was so positioned as to allow guns on its two faces to fire both up and down stream along the length of Short and Gillingham Reaches. By 1698 Gillingham fort was armed with forty culverins and ten demi-culverins, which were mainly to protect a new chain serving as a boom across the River Medway between Gillingham and Hoo Ness Island. This replaced the one that had been laid down in 1668.

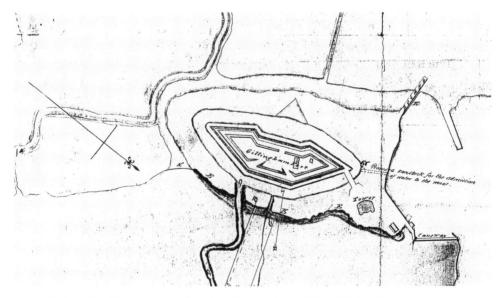

Ground plan of Gillingham Fort showing the position of the additional gun battery that was constructed on the north-east side of the fortress.

The remains of Cockhamwood Fort, also built after the Dutch raid as an additional defence of the Medway and located on the right bank of the Medway opposite Gillingham Fort. It was designed to crossfire with the guns of the fortress, so completely securing Gillingham Reach from enemy attack.

A more detailed view of Cockhamwood Fort. Constructed between 1669 and 1670, this recent photograph shows the still surviving lower-tier gun emplacements that would have housed powerful guns known as culverins.

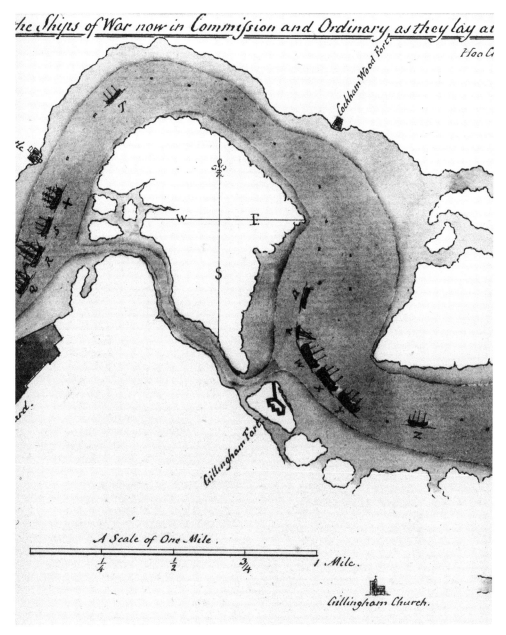

An early eighteenth-century plan of the River Medway showing the relative positions of Cockhamwood Fort and Gillingham Fortress. Vessels shown are naval warships moored in the river, a common sight in Gillingham Reach during the eighteenth century and for a great many years after.

A reminder of the battle fought off Gillingham can be seen in the village of Upnor at the house of Admiral Monck, whose last service for the country was to command some of the defences hastily put together to defend the Medway against the Dutch. His house is to be seen on the left of this photograph.

Having passed the village of Gillingham, the Dutch might well have gone on to destroy the dockyard, but two further factors now came into play. First, opposite St Mary's Island stood Upnor Castle, the only sizeable permanent defensive structure still able to resist the Dutch. Secondly, having now been in the Medway for several days there was the increasing risk of being cut off by an English fleet, which at one time had offered little threat through being some distance away in the North Sea but might now be heading in their direction. Realising that it would be necessary to capture the castle, so causing even more delay, it was decided to concentrate on the ships moored between Gillingham and the castle. Destroying *Royal James*, *Royal Oak* and *Loyal London*, sizeable battleships that failed to put up any real fight, the Dutch, at this point, took the decision to sail back into the Thames where they would have a better chance of surviving an encounter with any large fleet of English warships. In the event no such encounter took place, with the Dutch returning to their home ports having scored a considerable victory that placed them in a good position when a peace treaty was finally concluded just a few weeks later.

Evidence of that bitterly fought battle off Gillingham was to emerge some 200 years later. This was at a time when the dockyard at Chatham was undergoing a massive extension programme that would create the three basins and four new dry docks (later increased to five) along the length of St Mary's Creek. For the purpose of creating those three new basins, in total nearly 70 acres in extent, the creek that divided the island from the mainland had to be dug out and widened, with each of the three basins formed out of a deepened and widened waterway. In 1872, while undertaking this work, contractors uncovered the hull of a vessel burnt to the waterline. Almost certainly it was *Mathias*, one of the guardships that had been moored in a position close by the chain as part of its defence. While nowadays everything possible would have been done to preserve the remains, a rare example of a seventeenth-century warship that showed just how such ships were built, *Mathias* was simply photographed, with drawings made of her skeletal outline, and then covered over. She now lies buried somewhere beneath Basin 3.

DID YOU KNOW?
The arms of Charles I, which once adorned the stern of *Royal Charles*, the English flagship captured by the Dutch off Gillingham and towed across the North Sea to the Netherlands, are still preserved and on public display at the Rijksmuseum, a Dutch national museum, in Amsterdam. Following her capture and removal to the Netherlands, *Royal Charles* served as a popular tourist attraction, a reminder of the Dutch victory gained off Gillingham, with the vessel eventually scrapped but her stern carvings retained for posterity.

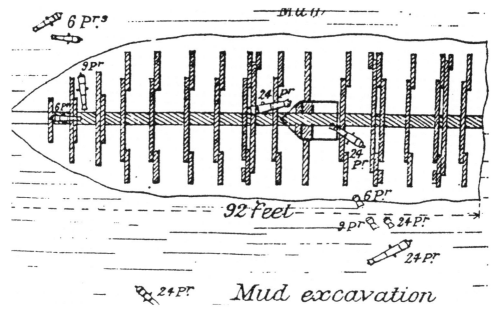

A copy of a drawing made in 1872 of the remains of a ship discovered in St Mary's Creek while excavation work for the dockyard extension was underway. If it was *Mathias*, as is commonly supposed, then she is of Dutch construction, being a former Dutch East Indiaman named *Geldersche Ruiter* that had been captured in 1665 and renamed *Mathias*.

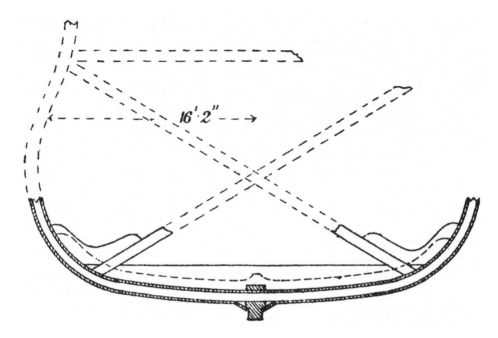

The midship section of the vessel uncovered in 1872. Burnt to the waterline, the dotted lines represent the probable form of the midship section.

A photograph taken in 1872 showing the ship uncovered during excavation work on the dockyard extension – the vessel lay near the east entrance to St Mary's Creek under a deposit of 15 feet of mud. Of oak construction, she was double-fastened with treenails and iron bolts.

3. Gillingham's Hidden Inhabitants

According to the first official national population census (undertaken in March 1801) Gillingham had a total of 4,135 inhabitants, of which 2,025 were male and 2,110 were female. As for how that population was gainfully employed, 600 were in trade and 132 in farming. Yet, in reality, these returns did not reflect the true nature of Gillingham's population at this point in time. In terms of numbers living in Gillingham, this was more than double, amounting to nearer 8,000 rather than 4,000.

So how had this discrepancy come about? Was it a lack of numeracy skills on the part of those counting the population or was it something more fundamental?

As it happens, those questions are easy to answer. Gillingham had a huge hidden population, with no effort made to include these individuals in the population count. As for the failure to include that hidden population, this was not the fault of Houstonne Radcliffe, the vicar of St Mary's who should have overseen this count, nor that of William Bagshaw, his lowly paid curate who probably did all of the spadework, with Radcliffe simply signing off the task. Their failure to get the numbers correct was a simple result of a government injunction that said that only those living in properly established family households or other parish institutions should be included. Not to be included, the government had declared, were seamen on board ships and those serving in the military. It is because of this injunction that figures for Gillingham's population in 1801 are entirely incorrect.

At the beginning of March 1801, when the census was undertaken, Gillingham was a military area, abundant in soldiers and naval seamen. On the Chatham side of the parish, St Mary's Barracks had been built during the 1780s to house soldiers brought there to construct and then man the defensive fortifications around the dockyard, originally known as the Cumberland Lines. Perhaps numbering as many as 2,000, not one of these residents was included in the census. In the River Medway, and also lying within the parish of Gillingham, were a number of warships, known as hulks, moored in both Gillingham Reach and Short Reach. These were old and obsolete vessels that had been converted in the yard at Chatham to house naval prisoners of war. Again, these prisoners were not included in the census returns submitted by Revd Radcliffe, although it is possible to be absolutely precise as to their numbers. In March 1801, at the time of the census, there were exactly 2,073 Dutch and French seamen living in Gillingham, incarcerated on board six prison hulks.

Of the Dutch prisoners, of which there were 587, many had been captured by the Royal Navy following the Battle of Camperdown, fought four years earlier. They were held on two hulks, *Sandwich* and *Buckingham* (both former warships that had seen many years of service), with one deck of *Buckingham* put aside for Dutch prisoners needing hospital care. A much larger group were the captured French seamen, 1,486 in total, who were housed on board *Rochester*, *Camperdown*, *Vryheid* and *Bristol*. Two of those ships, *Camperdown* and *Vryheid*, were former Dutch ships that had, alongside their crews, also been captured at the Battle of Camperdown, with *Camperdown*, once a proud warship carrying seventy-four guns and built in 1782 as *Jupiter*, now the hospital ship for French prisoners.

A view of the River Medway where the prisoners of war hulks were once moored.

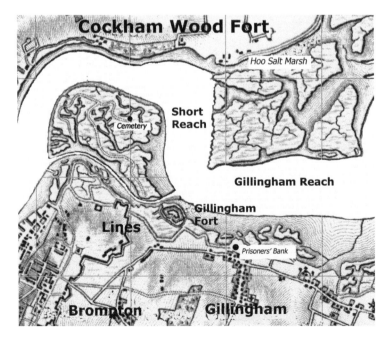

Map of the river showing the location of Gillingham and Short Reach and the two sites used by the Admiralty for the burial of those who died while on board the prison hulks.

Conditions on board these prison ships were truly appalling, made no better by the age of some of those vessels. *Sandwich*, the oldest, launched at Chatham dockyard in 1759, for the past eight years had served first as a hulk to hold press-ganged crews for British ships and now as a prison ship. She would eventually be broken up in 1810. Such vessels, deemed as unworthy for regular docking and maintenance, were damp throughout, a result of rainwater seeping in through each deck and the hull below the water line constantly leaking. Had *Sandwich* still been a regular warship, then she would have been docked and any necessary repairs carried out every three years. As a prison ship, she received no such privileges and was just allowed to rot. In summer, with each of the prison hulks holding more men than for which they had ever been designed, the high temperatures below decks was truly oppressive, especially as at night all of the port holes were sealed shut to prevent any prisoner escaping. In winter, through the lack of any form of heating, and temperatures (this being in the midst of the 'little ice age') often plummeting to temperatures well below freezing point, the coldness must have been unimaginable. Not surprisingly, disease and illness were rife, especially as the hulks were only allowed a minimal number of surgeons, resulting in treatment given to only a few of the most deserving.

Apart from having to deal with these extremes of temperature and fighting off disease and illness, the prisoners had to fight off boredom, many resorting to gambling as a means of passing away the time. Few, of course, had money, so all that could be wagered was the clothing they wore and their daily ration of food. The unlucky ended up eating very little or lacking any warm clothing to see them through those bitter winter nights. To try and bring about an end to such activities, the officers in charge of each of the hulks were instructed to keep a full record of all clothing issues, with no man to be allowed replacement clothes unless he could prove they required replacing through constant wear.

Some idea of the conditions under which the prisoners in the hulks had to live can be gained from a visit to the Guildhall Museum, Rochester, where an outstanding below-deck layout of a Gillingham prison hulk has been created. (Courtesy of the Guildhall Museum, Rochester)

William Burnett, a naval surgeon who later rose to become the Royal Navy's chief physician, was charged during the early winter of 1814 with overseeing the care arrangements for all seamen in the River Medway, including prisoners held on board the hulks moored off Gillingham. During that time Burnett, ignoring all risk to his own health, successfully brought an end to a typhoid fever epidemic that had claimed the lives of several hundred prisoners prior to his arrival. He later sailed as senior medical advisor to a Russian fleet that had overwintered in the Medway prior to sailing to St Petersburg. On arrival in St Petersburg, and for his work on saving the lives of many Russian seamen who had succumbed to typhoid fever during their stay in the Medway, he was awarded the Imperial Order of Saint Alexander Nevsky by Tsar Alexander I. More on Burnett while overseeing naval medical arrangements in the Medway can be found in *Secret Chatham*, a companion volume to *Secret Gillingham*.

A further burden suffered by those prisoners was that of receiving, even if they did not gamble it away, the provisions for which they were entitled. Merchants who supplied the food and the prison guards who stored the food frequently creamed off what they could to sell elsewhere. Frequently merchants and guards colluded with each other to falsify the accounts that were later delivered to the Transport Board, the department of the Admiralty that was responsible for the care of prisoners. Sometimes, also, essential provisions were held back from being distributed for the purpose of punishing the prisoners for any rules that they might have broken. Once such incident occurred on board *Rochester* in 1796

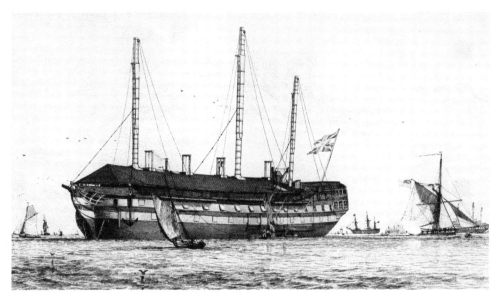

A view of a hulked warship, similar to those used to house prisoners of war, seen here moored in Gillingham Reach.

when for a period of six months the soap ration, which was set at 2 oz per man per week, was completely withheld for nine months. Apparently, some 600 lbs of soap had been stolen from the storeroom and the ration withheld from the prisoners because it was claimed, without any apparent evidence, that they had been responsible for the theft.

Violence on board these hulks was also not uncommon, with prisoners attacking one of the guards or fighting among themselves. The prison hulk *Sampson*, a former two-decked warship that was brought to Gillingham Reach as a prison hulk in March 1808 together with *Irresistible*, seemed particularly prone to such outbreaks. In March 1813, Louis Marquest, a native of Dijon who had been held on board *Sampson*, was sentenced to be hanged on Penenden Heath, following a trial at Maidstone in which he was found guilty of murdering fellow prisoner George Valiant. Almost a year later in February 1814, John Ashbee, a marine guarding the prisoners, was stabbed by Andre Mignott, a French prisoner, with the latter brought before a court in Rochester. Between those two events, in October 1813 a duel was fought between two French prisoners on board *Sampson*. Benoit Robert, having conceived himself insulted by Jacques Sotron, insisted that they should fight. Having no weapons, they unriveted a pair of scissors, to which they attached the blades to two sticks, each around a yard long. It was with these implements that they fought; Sotron inflicting a mortal wound upon his adversary, and for which a coroner's jury gave a verdict of self-defence.

The dampness and overcrowding of these vessels, combined with the extremes of temperature, poor diet and such punishments as the withholding of soap, ensured that morbidity and mortality rates were alarmingly high. Epidemics frequently broke out, with typhus and smallpox not uncommon. In March 1801, at the time of the census in Gillingham, nearly one-third of all French prisoners were suffering some form of illness – all attended by a single surgeon. Slightly healthier, possibly because of being fewer in number and leading to less crowding, were the Dutch. The hospital ship assigned to them, *Sandwich*, recorded only thirty-nine (6.7 per cent) receiving medical treatment.

In the case of death, burials, whether French or Dutch, at first took place in the grounds of the parish churchyard of St Mary's with two Dutch seamen, Cornelius Warbeck and Jan Willbrand, recorded as being buried here in 1797. Later, as a result of the high-mortality rate, the Admiralty decided that burials should take place on ground nearer to where the hulks were moored, with burials of prisoners from hulks in Short Reach taking place on St Mary's Island and those from hulks moored in Gillingham Reach taken for burial at Prisoners' Bank, a marshy island on the Gillingham side of the river facing onto Gillingham Reach.

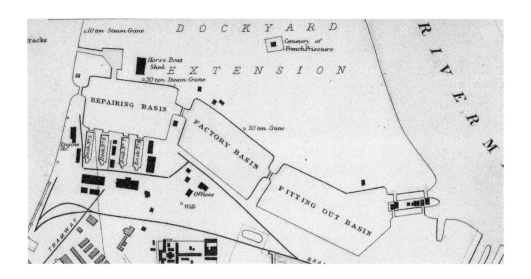

Above: A late nineteenth-century map of St Mary's Island showing the exact location of where the French prisoners of war were buried in relation to the subsequently built dockyard basins.

Left: Before French and Dutch prisoners of war were buried on the marshes on the Gillingham shoreline, some prisoners were buried in the parish churchyard of St Mary's (Grange Road Cemetery).

Those prisoners who were in a reasonable state of health were soon to find themselves returning to either the Netherlands or France as a result of a temporary peace treaty signed on 1 October 1801. Specifically, the treaty stated that 'all the prisoners made on one side and the other, as well by land as by sea, and the hostages carried off, or delivered up during the war, and up to the present day, shall be restored without ransom in six weeks at the latest.' Prior to that, the prisoners held in the hulks lying off Gillingham had an unpredictable future, not knowing how long they would be incarcerated, but with the occasional hope of being sent home as part of a general exchange of prisoners between those held in Britain and those held by the nations she was fighting. Those selected for exchange were supposed to be prioritised by incapacitation through war wounds or sickness, followed by those who had been longest in the hulks. But it did not always work like that. Some prisoners were able to bribe those who were drawing up the names of those to be exchanged, pushing those more deserving further down the list.

For those who believed themselves unlikely to be exchanged, another possible route home was to escape. As the prisoners were seamen, they were often skilled in the use of small craft. Once a successful break had been made, such prisoners often attempted to steal a local fishing boat that could then be sailed out into the Thames. Eventually, if their luck held out, they might get across the Channel to France. Three French officers certainly achieved this in early 1811, using a fishing boat taken from Gillingham. Unfortunately for one of them he was captured a few weeks later: a privateer that he now commanded was captured in the Channel and the unfortunate former prisoner returned to the same hulk off Gillingham from which he had originally escaped. Occasionally, it might be possible to bribe someone on shore to assist getting out of the country, although for any one so doing, the penalties were severe. In March 1813, several individuals who were found guilty of helping French prisoners escape the country were not only imprisoned for two years but had also to stand in the stocks at Maidstone. In November 1810, three French prisoners from *Sampson* also managed to secure a Gillingham fishing boat, and successfully took her over to France.

To escape from a prison hulk in the first place required courage, skill, ingenuity and a huge amount of luck. One almost successful escape took place in February 1813: a group of six or seven prisoners helping unload a victualling vessel delivering fresh beef seized the master of the vessel and the boy of the vessel, who was below slinging beef, casting off the rope by which the beef boat was fastened to the hulk. Immediately hoisting sail, they proceeded down the Medway under a favourable wind. A number of shots were fired from several of the guards on the various hulks that were passed in Gillingham Reach. Unfortunately for them, as they did not know the river, they ran onto a mud shoal off Commodore Hard, grounding the vessel. Closely pursued, all were recaptured in minutes, and one of the prisoners was wounded in the thigh.

Sometimes, as a means of escape, prisoners simply attempted to swim ashore. Eighteen jumped overboard from the prison hulk *Rochester* in October 1808, with nine immediately recaptured but the other eleven successfully disappearing. In 1812, a similar attempt by a Danish prisoner on board another prison hulk off Gillingham, ended when he drowned in the Medway.

As well as exchanging prisoners, whenever possible large groups were transferred from the prison hulks to prisons on land, of which both Dartmoor and Normans Cross had been built to accommodate an increasing number of prisoners taken by the Royal Navy at sea. As with the hulks, these land prisons were also administered by the Admiralty. Following the renewal of war in 1803, Emperor Napoleon refused to exchange prisoners, leading to an ever-increasing number having to be held in the hulks. Matters were made even worse from June 1812 onwards when war also broke out with the USA – even more enemy seamen now brought to the hulks off Gillingham. Helping relieve this situation was the building of the land prisons. Every so often, groups of prisoners would be taken from the hulks lying off Gillingham to these new prisons, but soon another batch of new arrivals would appear in the hulks.

WHEREAS the Commiffioners for conducting His Majefty's Tranfport Service, and for the Care and Cuftody of   Officers and Sailors detained in ENGLAND, have been pleafed to grant   Leave to refide in   upon Condition, that   give   Parole of Honour, not to withdraw   from the Bounds prefcribed   there, without Leave for that Purpofe from the faid Commiffioners; that   will behave   decently, and with due Regard to the Laws of this KINGDOM, and alfo that will not, either directly or indirectly, hold any Correfpon-dence with   during   continuance in ENGLAND, but by fuch Letter or Letters as fhall be fhewn to the Agent to the faid Commiffioners, under whofe Care   or may be, in order to their being read, and approved by   Superiors;   do hereby de-clare, that   have given   Parole of Honour accordingly, and that   will keep it inviolably.
Dated at

Captured naval officers were given very different treatment to those of ordinary seamen. If prepared to give their parole of honour not to leave a certain prescribed area, which might include the village of Gillingham, they were given freedom to live outside of the hulks. Any dishonouring of the conditions of their parole would result in them being immediately imprisoned. As proof of being a prisoner on parole they were given this document, which would be suitably signed and dated. Should an officer who had given his parole successfully escape to his home country, this would do him no good, as that country, even though hostile to Britain, would immediately enforce his return to captivity.

The land once used by the Admiralty on Gillingham Marsh to bury those who died in the prisoner-of-war hulks moored in Gillingham Reach was acquired by the Rochester and Chatham Gas Light Company in 1818. This is an aerial view of that same piece of land, complete with gasworks, as it appeared in the 1920s.

The bodies of French and possibly some Dutch prisoners of war, from wars fought at the end of the eighteenth century and beginning of the nineteenth century, were buried on St Mary's Island and then removed in 1904 to a new site within the grounds of the chapel of the naval barracks, St George's Church, now the St George's Centre, in 1904. A memorial to those prisoners of war was erected over the site at the time of the remains being reburied.

Upon the defeat of Napoleon in 1814, all French prisoners were repatriated. This immediately freed up room in the land prisons that had been built, so allowing the only remaining prisoners, the Americans (the war against the USA did not end until February 1815), to be removed from the remaining hulks in the Medway. It was this that brought a final end to the use of these vessels to accommodate prisoners of war. By October 1814, of eleven prison hulks stationed a few months earlier in either Short or Gillingham Reach, only *Irresistible* was still present, with this ship decommissioned during the first week of November.

DID YOU KNOW?
Several intense winters occurred while the prisoner-of-war hulks were moored in the Medway off Gillingham, with the river frequently freezing over. The early winter of 1811 was one such occasion, with drifting snow as high as the hedge tops and roads out of Gillingham completely impassable. On board the prison ships, the pumps supplying drinking water froze, adding to prisoner discomfort, while a seaman on board one of those hulks, *Nassau*, fell overboard and, even though quickly rescued, died from the intense coldness

4. St Mary's Island: Once a Marshland Wilderness

During the third quarter of the nineteenth century, St Mary's Island was home to the nation's then largest civil engineering project, turning a troublesome stretch of marshland into an industrial complex that was to become the envy of the world. It was a project that took Chatham dockyard into Gillingham and created a major urban conurbation out of Gillingham that would come to house thousands of dockyard workers and their families. Also thrown into this same conurbation were the numerous commercial enterprises, shops, buildings and places of entertainment that were necessary to sustain this major growth in population.

A general view across St Mary's Island as it is today and looking towards the three basins that were created out of St Mary's Creek.

That St Mary's Island had been proving troublesome was because of two factors – one not realised at the time and the other very much a concern. The first, not grasped at the time, resulted from the island having an extensive area of freshwater marshland known as Finsborough Marsh. Here lay various stagnant pools of water, the ideal breeding ground for mosquitoes, including the anopheline variety that served as the vector for the spreading of malaria. In spring and autumn these blood-sucking pests spread the disease, with those contracting it often having to take to their beds for several weeks. This was the island's hidden menace. At that time, it was not realised that this disease, often referred to as 'the autumnals' but better known as ague, was actually spread by those irritating creatures who took to settling on exposed skin at night while the victim lay asleep. In tropical climes, malaria usually spells death, but in the milder climate of north Kent it produces only debilitation, with death only resulting when combined with another serious illness as the body is unable to fight off both at the same time.

Another, and much more visible, reason for St Mary's Island proving troublesome was the waterway that separated the island from the mainland – St Mary's Creek. The creek was a major cause of mud accumulating in front of the dockyard at Chatham, necessitating the constant dredging of the river. If this stretch of water was blocked, the process of mud being taken from the island and flowing into the river would be stopped. Given that this, in turn, would increase both the size and value of the island, it would also be logical for the Admiralty to purchase St Mary's Island for future expansion of the dockyard.

Prior to the Admiralty acquiring St Mary's Island, it was viewed as being of limited value because of being primarily marshy, some saltwater marshland and some, through the erection of mud embankments, freshwater. It nevertheless had a small population, possibly as many as thirty or forty living on St Mary's Island, for in the year 1814 there were eleven tenements on the island. Appropriately, given that life on the island must have been fairly remote, five of these tenements were collectively known as 'Tom All-Alones'. As to ownership of the island, Elizabeth Strover, a widow of Brompton, owned 25 acres and Robert Simmons of Rochester a further 7 acres. It is unclear as to who at that time owned the rest of the island. That the land was being put to some sort of use must be assumed by the fact that Elizabeth Strover was leasing her 18 acres of freshwater marshland to Thomas Baseden, almost certainly for the grazing of sheep during the winter months.

A decision to purchase 25 acres of the Island was taken by the Admiralty in July 1819, with its purchase enabled by an Act of Parliament that was passed in 1821. At the time, the primary reason was to acquire this land before it took on increased value, with it to be immediately used for the storage of timber and depositing large amounts of mud dredged from the river. The stopping up of the creek was not immediately contemplated and it was also recognised that Rochester Bridge was probably an even greater contributor to the silting of the river. This resulted from the huge stone supports (known as starlings) reducing the flow of the current as it passed under the bridge, so inhibiting the natural scouring of the river that would have resulted from an unrestricted flow of water at this point.

While prisoners of war had, at one time, been buried on the island, it was now convicts who were being brought over to the island, but for a very different reason. These were men who had been convicted of criminal offences, coming to the island to perform menial tasks that were given to them as part of a regime of punishment through hard labour. The specific task was that of emptying the barges that contained the dredged mud from the river.

The decision to convert the island into a massive extension to the already existing dockyard was finally taken during the 1850s. The Admiralty, through a further Act of Parliament, purchased the entire island as it had been decided that St Mary's Creek could usefully be converted into a series of three enclosed basins for the repair, maintenance and fitting out of warships, with the island itself providing much of the land needed for additional workshops, a factory and stores. To allow for this work to begin, a further Act of Parliament had to be obtained to allow the Admiralty the right to purchase the rest of the island and also to block from public use the creek that separated the island from the mainland. This same Act also dealt with the need to compensate the mayor and aldermen and Company of Free Dredgers of the city of Rochester for the destruction of the fishery in the creeks.

An interior view of the convict prison that was built to accommodate those employed in the construction of the St Mary's Island extension to the dockyard.

This obelisk in the Grange Road cemetery commemorates John Smith, a one-time superintendent of the Chatham Dockyard Division of the Metropolitan Police. It was while he was serving in this role that the convicts on St Mary's Island were employed on the extension of the dockyard, with Smith informed in September 1876 of a possible attack on the prison to release a number of Irish Republicans who were being held at the prison. It was feared that the prison would be attacked by a mob, but in the event the threat came to nothing.

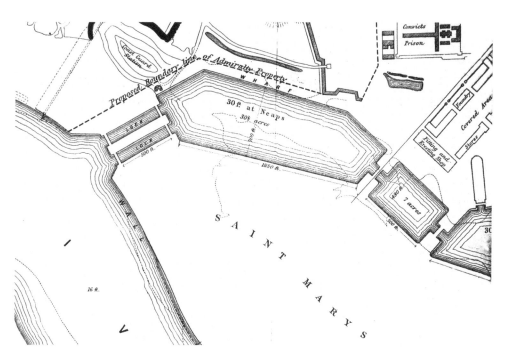

An outline plan showing an early design for the basins that were to run the length of St Mary's Creek.

Prior to the necessary excavation and construction work beginning, a force of labourers had to be recruited; and what better source for this than the continuing use of convicts? After all, it was only necessary for them to be given a derisory wage, which they would receive on the expiration of their sentence. In not having to meet the going wage for the employment of labourers and other skilled workers, this would also help pay the costs of maintaining the prisoners and the wardens who were needed to guard them. Still housed in convict hulks on the river, the first task they were given was building a new prison on land – this was sited to the south of St Mary's Creek where the campus of the Universities at Medway is now located (formerly HMS *Pembroke*). Following completion of the prison, convicts were next given the task of building a river wall and embankment. The estimated cost was £85,000 (£7.5 million today), with the course of the creek eventually to be transformed into the three large ship basins that still exist. At the same time as this work was underway, further groups of convicts, frequently numbering as many as 1,000, were engaged in the complete draining of the marshes on St Mary's Island, building the land up by an additional 8 feet, with sure foundations also dug for the numerous projected buildings. A further task given to the convicts was that of preparing and then operating a 21-acre brick field built at the north end of St Mary's Island. This produced most of the bricks used in the extension and is said to have been responsible for the manufacture of 110 million bricks by March 1875.

The first phase of the extension was completed in 1871, which was marked by the official opening of the Repairing Basin (later Basin 1) in June of that year. This is the basin standing immediately opposite Upnor, and, at that time, built with an entrance into the

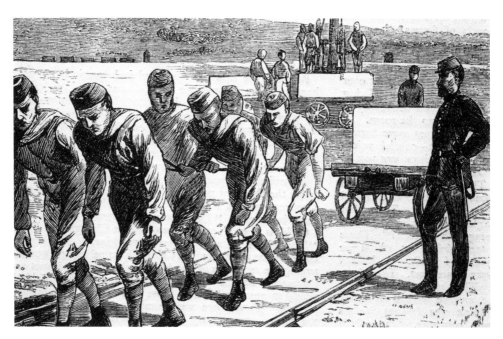

Convicts undertaking heavy labouring duties in connection with the building of the dockyard extension, with a warder standing nearby to ensure that they kept up a good pace of work.

In the later years of the extension, as seen in this photograph, prisoners were used less and certainly not in the skilled work of driving locomotives.

Work on Dock 5, the first of the dry docks to be completed, and which is on the south side of the Repairing Basin (Basin 1) seen at the time of its completion.

Following completion of Dock 5 came Dock 6.

Seen here in January 1878, work is underway on the Fitting Out Basin (Basin 3), which is viewed here from St Mary's Island.

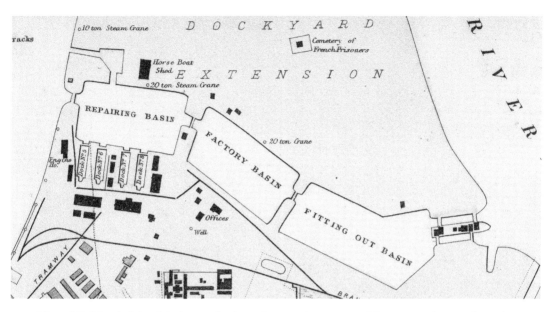

Map of St Mary's Island dating to the late nineteenth century, with construction work on the extension more or less complete. Shown on this map is both the location of the original French cemetery that was used to bury prisoners of war who died on the hulks and the site of the convict prison (lowermost middle of map) that was built to the south of the island.

River Medway. Next was the Factory Basin (later Basin 2) and finally, in 1883, the Fitting Out Basin (later Basin 3). It was this latter basin that also provided a primary entry into the Medway through the caisson gates of the Bull's Nose – so named because of its shape. Although in this later construction work continued use was made of convict labour, the savings were not as great as had originally been expected. For this reason, much more of the work on both Basins 2 and 3 involved a large proportion of contract labour, with the employment of convicts reduced.

Once the work on building the extension was complete there was no longer any need for the prison. The building was demolished and the area it once occupied acquired by the Admiralty for construction of a naval barracks, which allowed ratings previously accommodated in hulks that, in common with the prison and convict hulks, had also been moored in the Medway. While life might not have been over comfortable for those ratings, their hulks were certainly better maintained and less regimented than those of the convicts. Once built, the new barracks created a more comfortable environment, providing not just more spacious accommodation but also recreation areas, a gymnasium and a large parade ground. While not built on St Mary's Island, ratings attached to the barracks were frequently brought there – an island still separate from the mainland by the three basins. In turn, these basins were straddled by a series of bridges, these formed over caissons that sealed each basin but were floated to one side when a ship needed to pass through.

A general view of the naval barracks, seen shortly after first occupation in 1903. While not on the island of St Mary's, the barracks has a close association with the island through being built on the site of the former convict prison and a large part of the island having been given over to recreational areas for those in the barracks who were either under training or waiting to join a ship.

One of the depot ships that provided accommodation for naval ratings prior to the construction of the Royal Naval Barracks.

Royal Naval Barracks, Dry Canteen. Facilities at the barracks was a considerable improvement over depot ships. Construction of the new barracks began in May 1897, with building work substantially completed by December 1902. Total accommodation at that time was for 4,742 officers and men with emergency wartime accommodation given as 7,720.

An unusual scene in the Royal Naval Barracks: a re-enactment of the navy's role in suppressing the Boxer uprising in China. This re-enactment, with the public invited on a day when the barracks was open to all, was put on soon after the official opening of the barracks.

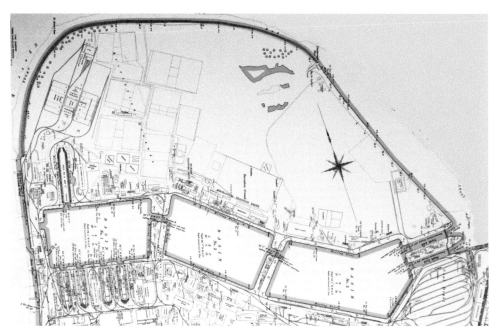

Map of St Mary's Island, originally dating to 1911 but updated in 1942, showing the limited use that was really being made of the island other than a cluster of buildings to the north of the three basins.

A modern-day view of the parade ground of the former Royal Naval Barracks, HMS *Pembroke*.

Naval motifs abound within the former naval barracks, now the campus of the Universities at Medway.

From that time onwards, the story of St Mary's Island is very much the story of Chatham dockyard: a continual movement of ships into the various basins, with the dockyard needing a massively increased workforce to service naval ships, whether in need of repair, maintenance or fitting out. On St Mary's Island, apart from the construction of a single dry dock on the north-west side of Basin 1 (Dock 9) and lines of workshops and stores alongside all three basins, much else was left undeveloped. Instead, a substantial part of the island saw either no development or was given over for recreational purposes, such as tennis, cricket and football, for use by ratings of the naval barracks. With a gradual reduction in the size of the Royal Navy following the ending of the Second World War, questions began to be asked as to the future of the dockyard. The establishment of a Nuclear Refit Centre alongside Basin 1 seemed to secure Chatham's future, but only until 25 June 1981 when it was announced in Parliament that the dockyard would close, an event that followed just three years later. While it was an act that ripped the heart out of the Medway Towns, St Mary's Island and the three basins running along the former creek were seen as integral to the repairing of the damage that had been done through being designated as an area for new residential and commercial accommodation, leading to the construction of several hundred new homes and the necessary supporting infrastructure. While the former Basins 1 and 2 have seen adaption to leisure use, Basin 3 was taken over by the Medway Ports Authority as a commercial port.

DID YOU KNOW?

In 1851, when the project to build the naval extension was only in very early planning stages, the population of Gillingham stood at 9,321. By 1891, when the work on transforming St Mary's Island into the central feature of the Medway military-industrial complex, the population of Gillingham had seen a threefold increase – totalling 27,872 by that year. Most were living in houses that were squeezed as close as possible to the dockyard and, in particular, the new Gillingham Gate.

The Finsborough slipway, once used for repairing lighters used for taking materials and dockyards 'mateys' from the dockyard out to naval ships moored in the Medway.

Millennium Sculpture, which stands alongside the Finsborough slipway.

Looking across Basin 1, originally the Repairing Basin, towards St Mary's Island.

Today, berthed in Basin 1, along with pleasure yachts and other boats, are several historic vessels including *MT Kent*, a harbour tug built for J. P. Knight of Rochester. *VIC 96*, the vessel to the right, was launched in 1945 as an Admiralty Victualling Inshore Craft (VIC), serving at Sheerness Dockyard between 1945 and 1959.

5. Health Resort

Hard to believe, and certainly one of its best-kept secrets, but for a brief period during the early nineteenth century Gillingham was well on the way to becoming a significant rival to the pleasures of Margate, Ramsgate or even Brighton. Its advantages as an up and coming health resort were quite considerable: within relatively easy reach of London, able to offer much in the way of entertainment, and the waters of the River Medway were regarded as clean and wholesome. As for accommodating the many visitors that began descending on the area, Brompton was the place to stay, the small hamlet within the parish of Gillingham viewed as having tavern accommodation that was described 'as good and respectable'. What more could anyone demand?

Behind this sensational development was a belief in the health-giving qualities of seawater, with total immersion advocated by those with a medical background. A summer spent bathing every day in the Medway at Gillingham would be a sure guarantee of future good health while also thought to cure a whole list of illnesses that included not just tuberculosis but the much-feared cholera. In Margate, which admittedly did have a bit of an edge over Gillingham, the Royal Sea Bathing Hospital had pioneered the use of open-air treatment for patients, concentrating on those suffering from tubercular complaints with, so it was claimed, remarkable results. Those financing and handsomely profiting from the new resort at Gillingham doubtless hoped that here, too, such a hospital might well be established.

It was in May 1837 that this group of individuals, through the issuing of £2 shares to finance the venture, finalised their plans. Choosing a situation close by Gillingham Fort,

Somewhere in this stretch of water, but probably slightly further inland than where the beach currently exists, was the location of the Floating Bath Establishment as created in 1837. Its exact location, other than being somewhere near Gillingham Fort and the present-day Gillingham Pier, is unknown.

and therefore not so far from the present-day Gillingham Pier, a floating bath designed to be used for bathing in the Medway was purchased for use by the best of London society. Floating baths at this time were highly popular and certainly the easiest and cheapest way of creating a health resort where none had previously existed. A floating bath was formed out of an area of water around 30 square feet, enclosed by upright planks sunk into the river bed with two flat-topped floating boats moored on either side of these planks. The floor at one end would have been around 3 feet underwater and the other around 8 feet, with the planks all around having gaps that were sufficiently narrow as to protect bathers from being drawn under the boats, while the frame was sufficiently open to let currents of water pass through. Upon the decks of the two boats changing rooms and other facilities for dispensing drinks and food were constructed. As for the need for propriety in age of delicate behaviour, no mixed bathing was permitted, with men and women given separate hours in which they were permitted to enter the establishment and take to the water.

So successful was the venture that shareholders, at the end of the first season, the summer of 1837, received a 10 per cent return on their investment. Not surprisingly there was a general agreement at a meeting held in the parish meeting room of St Mary's Church that the existing facilities should be added to, with a decision taken to raise a building on shore for warm baths. This would not only attract more visitors but allowed the season to be extended by several months.

To further encourage visitors to the new sea bathing establishment, much was also made of various attractions in the area, with Gillingham seen as much more than a resort just for bathing. One journalist, in bestowing the virtues of the area, made a point of referring to the numerous military exercises performed by troops housed in the barracks in Gillingham – those of St Mary's and Brompton. During the summer months, he explained, the soldiers of the two garrisons 'may be seen every day engaged in the performance of various military evolutions on the Lines'. Such activity, he assured any visitor to Gillingham, especially if a 'lover of military parade and pomp', would be fully gratified.

A bonus for those visiting the Floating Bath Establishment was that of being close to the Cumberland Lines and the frequent military displays that took place each summer. Typical, although dating to 1851, is this fine display of military presence on the Lines, which brought spectators from far and wide. In the near distance, and to the right, Gillingham Fort is seen, the approximate site of the bathing establishment.

It was not always necessary to travel as far as the Cumberland Lines to appreciate the skills of the military. This underwater explosion was set off by the Royal Engineers at a point immediately off the Gillingham shoreline.

Horse racing was another attraction, with a two-day event held within Gillingham on the summit of the Cumberland Lines during the first week of September. Again, the wealthy and fashionable were always represented, with many dukes, barons and knights of the realm always putting in an appearance. From the surrounding area, large crowds would also descend on Gillingham for the event, brought there by omnibuses travelling from Sittingbourne, Faversham, Gravesend and Canterbury. Adding to the entertainment, each race day evening witnessed a firework display, with the larger local taverns and inns putting on balls and other festive proceedings.

The scene on the first day of the races, held in September 1837, was fully described by a correspondent of the *Kentish Mercury*:

From early hour of the morning, vehicles of every description arrived in rapid succession from all parts of the country – first, the farmer's cart and broad wheeled waggon, decorated with boughs and evergreens, and filled with the smiling faces of rustic Kentish beauties, and their sweethearts and husbands. These were followed by the dog carts and barrows of the itinerant vendors of fruit and walking sticks, oysters and ginger beer, salmon and gingerbread, sausages, and songs [3 yards for halfpenny] &c &c. Then came the cart of the farmer, the buggy of the tradesman, the four wheeled chaise of the retired family man, the close and open carriages of the aristocracy, and posts and four, the pinks and tulips of sporting society. Each took up his station according to his rank or, rather, according to the rank in which his pocket chose for him.

The magnificence of the course was also remarked upon:

> Much has been said and written on the beauties and excellence of the courses of Epsom and Ascot, but we doubt very much if the gentlemen who have so strongly eulogised on those places ever visited the Lines of Chatham, or they must have acknowledged that the course here [although not as extensive as many others] for lofty and extensive views, of rich and beautiful scenery, is superior to any other course in England.

To the spectacle of military manoeuvres on the Cumberland Lines and annual horse racing, Gillingham could also offer the solemnity and solitude of the countryside and the nearby spectacle of one of the world's largest naval dockyards. Warships moored in the river combined with the frequent comings and goings of steamers offered an endless round of entertainment that might soon place Gillingham at the forefront of all the nation's seaside resorts. But then disaster struck...

On the night of 30 September 1842, at the end of the establishment's sixth successful season, a severe storm took its toll. High winds and unexpected high waves filled the flat boats with water, with the whole complex sinking into 20 feet of water. Within hours the whole thing was a complete wreck. The stakeholders, who in that year had received a return of 15 per cent on their original investment, had by now almost made an overall profit, but were reluctant to reinvest. Aware that the same could happen to any future floating baths establishment, they decide to keep what they had and look elsewhere as to where to invest their money. The result for Gillingham was that it failed to become that much fancied seaside resort. Indeed, the waters of the River Medway were handed back to local residents, and they, and only they, continued to swim here each year.

The popular beach at the Strand, seen here during the 1930s.

And, again, in the 1950s.

Eventually, but not until 1896, Thomas Cuckow, a local baker, took up the challenge of creating another open-air bathing pool close to the sight of that earlier floating bath establishment. This was even less refined – nothing more than a depression immediately above the high-water mark. It was certainly not designed to attract the London crowds, especially as it was overshadowed by the nearby gasworks. Nevertheless, it proved a popular local attraction, with improvements only coming in 1920 when chlorination and filtration units were added together with wooden changing rooms. In tandem with these improvements this waterside area of Gillingham (now known as the Strand) gained, with the help of the borough council, a paddling pool, bandstand, car park, an ice-cream parlour with deck chairs for hire by those wishing to soak up the sun. In time, of course, numerous other improvements have followed, including frequent improvements to a children's play park and the introduction of a miniature railway line.

DID YOU KNOW?
As it was redeveloped by Gillingham Borough Council during the interwar years, the Strand was so popular during the summer months that it was attracting as many as 12,000 visitors in any one day. Admission rates to the open-air swimming pool in those days was 4*d* for adults and 1*d* for children.

THE BEACH, GILLINGHAM.

A further view of the Strand in the 1930s.

Although lazing on the beach alongside the Medway is not as popular as it might once have been, its emptiness on this occasion is explained by this being a wintertime picture, when many of the attractions of the Strand were closed until the following year. However, in the sizzling summer of 2019, hundreds, if not thousands, descended on the Strand, with lengthy queues forming outside the pool.

6. Queen Jezebel and the Tower of the Jezreelites

Gillingham once possessed a truly mysterious landmark, visible for miles around: a giant cube-like structure adorned with motifs and projecting turrets that offered few clues as to its purpose or origin. Roofless and with unglazed windows, it stood on ground sided by Rainham Road to the south and Canterbury Street to the east. For residents travelling back to Gillingham by road, whether from one of the seaside resorts in east Kent or a business trip to London, an early glimpse of the tower, often from some distance, was a sure and comforting sign that home would shortly be reached and the day's journey was coming to a close.

Demolished in 1961, it was a building never completed for its true purpose, but with its presence still commemorated in an area of Gillingham known as Jezreel. The tower itself, always known as Jezreel's Tower, was named after its creator, James Jershom Jezreel. Not that Jezreel was his real name, JJJ having been born James Rowland White. However, as the founder of a new religious movement that had as its core belief that God was about to replace the present order 'by the glorious reign of the Lord Jesus', he required a more suitable name. As a self-proclaimed messenger of God, Jezreel was deemed appropriate. It was taken from the Old Testament and referred to a site in Lower Galilee where a battle had been fought between good and evil. It was here that Queen Jezebel, a name with obvious overtones, was defeated, her fate that of being thrown from a tower – the tower of Jezreel.

It was in 1875 that the future JJJ first arrived on the local scene. A member of the 16th Regiment of Foot, he had recently been posted to Chatham, frequenting various religious meetings. Dissatisfied with the more established views of the Christian church, he took upon himself the mantle of a prophet, going on to establish the New and Latter House of Israel. Clearly he was a man possessed of a very persuasive character, gifted with untiring energy but seen as tyrannical in his rule. Those who knew him would describe him as a fine, broad-shouldered man, nearly 6 feet in height. Adding to his character as a prophet was that of JJJ having a long beard and hair that flowed to his shoulders – a style of appearance also adopted by his male followers.

Over the years this newly created movement was to gain considerable strength, aided by missionary workers. From Gillingham they took the teachings of JJJ far and wide, promising a guarantee of immortality in a forthcoming thousand-year reign of God. Many were encouraged to come to Gillingham where a community of several hundred had been established by the late 1870s. In having come to Gillingham, sect members previously in possession of property were urged to sell their worldly possessions so that the money received could be used for the good of the entire community. As it happens, a larger proportion of those proceeds appears to have been used personally by JJJ and those immediately around him to provide a somewhat comfortable lifestyle that included large amounts of alcohol and the finest of foods. Others of the sect – those who had provided the money – had to put up with cabbage, peas, beans and very little meat. Furthermore, while accommodated in special houses, they had to work for their keep, employed in a host of business ventures from which each had to donate one-tenth of their earnings. Any complaints would result in a reduction of food that members were allowed, with an elaborate and intrusive system of spying used to enforce the rules, making life quite intolerable for some.

By 1884 the New and Latter House of Israel, with so much money coming in from the faithful, had sufficient funds to finance a dynamic new project. This was construction of the massive turreted tower, originally referred to as 'Israel's Sanctuary', that was to serve as both a church and world headquarters of the new movement. Announcing that it was through a dream that God had commanded him to build the tower, JJJ laid down that it should, in appearance, replicate the shape of Jerusalem as described in the Book of Revelation. To this end, the tower would need to be 'foursquare' with 'the length and the breadth and the height of it ... equal'. JJJ was later to elaborate on this, writing that the building 'will be three storeys, 144 feet [44 m] square. Its subterranean passages will extend for miles. The holy of holies will form the topmost graft into the building, lit by a revolving electric light. It is to be the grandest building in the whole of these parts. The lower storey will contain twelve [printing] presses, the whole worked by a large steam engine ... the second and middle storey will be [the] great hall seating many thousands.'

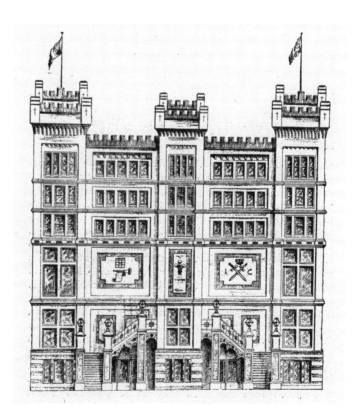

A drawing of the Jezreelite tower showing how it was supposed to look once completed.

The starting point was the purchase of a 6.25-acre plot of land alongside Rainham Road for £2,700 from the Rock Freehold Land Society. While some of this land was to be used for the grazing of a dairy herd, its centre point was to be the sanctuary tower. For the purpose of constructing that tower, Margetts of Chatham, a locally based firm of architects, were asked to provide the necessary architectural drawings. They apparently advised on the impossibility of constructing the tower to the exact specifications that JJJ gave, significantly modifying parts of the design and certainly not including the several miles of underground passages. However, they did incorporate into the design a sizeable circular-shaped assembly room that was to be entirely enclosed within the building and, through being windowless, would be lit both day and night by a huge lantern suspended from the ceiling. In the centre of this circular room a detached platform was to be erected for both preachers and choir that could be raised by hydraulic power from the floor below. JJJ's original idea had been for this platform to also revolve, but he was persuaded that the expense for this would be far too great.

It was just as the final plans had been confirmed, on 1 March 1885, that the first of many disasters struck. JJJ, a man who insisted that his followers abstain from drink, died of alcohol poisoning. This, in truth, was a double blow for the New and Latter House of Israel. Not only did his death finally reveal JJJ to be far from the unblemished character that many believed him to be, but his death somewhat undermined the promise of immortality

Jezreel's Temple, or Israel's Sanctuary as it was originally named, as it was when building work ceased in March 1888. The tower remained like this in appearance until 1905. Even though it lacked a roof to the top storey, it was still used by the sect. The ground floor contained several printing presses for the production of their monthly magazine, which was sent around the world. Seen on the outside of the building are symbols of the Jezreelite sect.

that all who joined the religious sect had been given. A power struggle within the sect followed, with later leaders taking an authoritarian attitude towards their followers while continuing to squander much of the accumulated wealth. Many began to leave the fold while others, due to their self-imposed poverty, could only look on in bewilderment.

Nevertheless, the remaining faithful, while dwindling in numbers, carried through on the project, with the foundation stone of the ambitious structure laid in September 1885. It was a building designed to play its full part in the new thousand-year reign of God, with no expense spared on its construction. The builders, James Gouge Naylor of Rochester, were only to use bricks of the best quality, together with vast amounts of iron and steel supporting girders, beams, columns and ribs to strengthen the building from within. Eager to make full use of the structure, even before it was completed, the printing presses were installed on the ground floor and religious tracts began to pour out for dissemination around the world. Then came one more disaster: the sect ran out of money and were unable to continue paying the builders. This was after £30,000 had already been paid out, with £20,000 needing to be found. All this was just as the roof was due to be set in place, a roof that would have been formed of concrete and asphalt. In March 1888 all construction work ceased and, with money owing to them, the builders took possession of the unfinished temple together with a row of adjacent shops and

Internally the building had great strength, through the use of a considerable number of iron girders and beams. This greatly added to the problem of the tower's later demolition.

cottages in Canterbury Street. This now placed the sect in the position of tenants, with the printing presses allowed to remain and the ground floor of the tower, also used as a bakery and laundry.

The remaining members of the Jezreelite sect continued to disseminate their message of everlasting life and the coming reign of god in their monthly publication, *The Messenger of Wisdom and Israel's Guide.* While those printing presses continued to whirl on the ground floor of the unfinished tower, the tower was sold by Naylor to a property developer, Bowdage, Pedley and Tanton. They planned to turn the tower into a factory. This was in 1905, with the sect told that they must now completely vacate the property together with the houses that the sect occupied along Canterbury Street. This, as it happens, was an area undergoing considerable change, with land here having taken on a greatly increased value. In part, this resulted from a new electric tram line that had been built along Watling Street, but also because of a demand for new homes created by the expanding dockyard. While the tower had originally been surrounded by open fields, it was now surrounded by housing. Of these changes, a correspondent of the Tunbridge Wells-based *Kent & Sussex Courier* (23 June 1905) wrote:

> The Tower is still much in evidence its unfinished condition, and the row of buildings in front of the Tower on the main road I found still occupied by the Jezreelites, but the neighbourhood has completely changed. There are now hundreds of homes on the land immediately surrounding the Tower, all of which are occupied, and others being built. In fact, a new town has sprung up.

The central assembly room seen sometime around 1905, with an area in the centre that was reserved for a hydraulically powered platform that would have been raised from the floor below and upon which would have been preachers and choir.

This correspondent then went on to explain the position of the Jezreelites and of their now being required to vacate both the tower and the adjoining buildings in which some members of the sect were housed, going on to add:

Talking the matter over with a friend, I said it was a wonder to me that there were no shops there, and inquired why the Jezreelites—who I learn are still there—did not utilise their row of buildings as shops, instead of having only one a kind of refreshment room? This appears do a very good trade in that line, and the profits derived would surely help them to finish the Tower. My friend then informed me that the Jezreelites were under notice to quit, not only the Tower but also the row of buildings and that by the end of July the inhabitants of Gillingham and Chatham will witness the strange sight of a steam crane on the top of the Tower levelling it to the second storey. The present owners intend roofing it in, and thus converting it into valuable premises for a factory. My friend also remarked that the tenements would then be converted into a row of useful and much-needed shops.

An attempt, in 1905, to level the tower to the second storey was only partially successful, leaving the building slightly shorter but still visible from many miles away.

The tower, again seen here in its final state before any demolition work was attempted, but without its top-storey roof. Open countryside abounds in an area now packed with housing – much was built shortly after this photograph was taken.

An aerial view of Gillingham dating to the late 1920s with Canterbury Street clearly visible and Jezreel's Tower in the bottom-left corner.

A further group of buildings once owned by the sect lined the top end of Canterbury Street, but were demolished in 2008. Built in 1886, they were originally used for instructing scholars in the 'true' faith.

Although work began on levelling the sanctuary tower to the second storey, it was not completed due to the builders going bankrupt. An attempt to sell the building a few years later also failed, with the Gillingham Co-operative Society acquiring, during the 1920s, all of the land and buildings that had once belonged to the Jezreelites, converting some of the premises along Canterbury Street into shops. As for the tower, although missing a few chunks from the finished but unroofed top storey, this continued to look out across the neighbouring countryside, a visible landmark that could be seen from as far away as the Isle of Grain and Sheerness. For a time, the interior of the tower was put to use as a hard tennis court, with grass courts in the field once used for the grazing of dairy cattle. While retaining the former Jezreelite buildings along Canterbury Street, the Co-operative Society in 1959 finally found a purchaser for the tower: a developer who set about its complete demolition. For many in Gillingham, this was a sad day. The tower was such an obvious landmark and one to which residents were fondly attached. Undeterred, even by a suggestion that the tower was protected by the curse of JJJ, demolition work proceeded, with the tower completely levelled to the ground by the spring of 1961. In its place came an electro-plating works owned initially by Smiths Signs and later by L. Robinson & Co. (Gillingham) Ltd. Today, with even the former Jezreelite buildings along Canterbury Street also now demolished and the land on which they stood under redevelopment, there are few clues, other than in the name of this area of Gillingham, as to the existence of the sect and their former tower.

DID YOU KNOW?
Rock Avenue, the road on the Chatham Hill side of the tower was named after the Rock Freehold Land Society. It was this society that sold land to the Jezreelites for construction of the tower and other buildings. The purpose of a freehold society, of which many were formed around the country, was to enable men with only limited capital to acquire freehold property and, in so doing, acquire the right to vote in parliamentary and local elections. They were part of a strategy undertaken by Liberal radicals to effect parliamentary reform.

A glimpse along the road leading towards Chatham would once have been dignified by an avoidable site of the unfinished Israel's Sanctuary.

Another view of the area close to the former Jezreel's Tower and so markedly different from the unbroken countryside that thrived on the southern side of the borough when the tower was built during the 1880s.

Jezreel is still the name given to this area of Gillingham despite the long disappearance of the sect and its landmark tower.

7. A Red-letter Day

When the Prince of Wales, the future Edward VII, first visited the Medway Towns in April 1875, Gillingham was not on his itinerary. On that occasion he was here to launch *Alexandria*, a massive new central battery timber-hulled iron-clad battleship. The royal train from Victoria took him to Chatham station where a horse-drawn carriage awaited him. This took him on to the dockyard by way of Railway Street and Dock Road before passing through Main Gate. To have taken him by way of Gillingham, would not, at that time, have impressed him, for although the dockyard now stretched into Gillingham, this part of the yard was still under construction. The same could also be said of the town of Gillingham as much of it was a building site, with hundreds of new homes under construction and continuous lines of streets beginning to emerge. Often built by their owners and future occupiers, and with the town lacking firm municipal authority at that time, these houses were beginning to take on a myriad of styles with a similar variation in quality. Many were clustered closest to the where the extension was being built – family homes for those employed in the dockyard.

The village of Gillingham as it appeared at the time of Edward VII's opening of the Royal Naval Hospital. It was a village still retaining a rustic charm and in total contrast to developments of Gillingham closer to the dockyard. The Olde Five Bells (later Five Bells) dates back to the seventeenth century, but the building was converted into flats in more recent years.

Helping the growth of Gillingham, or at least that part once known as New Brompton, was the arrival of the railway and the opening of New Brompton station in 1858, later New Brompton (Gillingham) and finally Gillingham station.

Gillingham railway station following a more recent revamping and updating of its entrance area, with the earlier 1930s entrance to be seen just beyond the new glass entrance area. It was from this station that the royal train collected the king following Edward VII's visit to the town in 1905.

Through the huddled and haphazard nature of that development, the parish of Gillingham was a strange contrast of frenetic urbanisation and rural bliss. On its eastern side, close to the river, where the parish church can still be found, farming folk were stoically going about their business while visitors from London were coming to this part of Gillingham for fresh air and rustic quiet, although not in the numbers once drawn to the short-lived bathing establishment. Gravitate further west, to the area of the parish that had at that time adopted the name of New Brompton, and where most of those houses were being built, that rustic idyll was very much of the past. New Brompton was a veritable town in the making. Unlike the original centre of the parish, it even had its own railway station, an important addition to the area that provided a further incentive for all this new house building.

Clearly, in style, name and aspiration, the two parts of Gillingham had little in common and would, for some time, continue to develop in directions that appeared almost diametrically opposed to each other.

In 1905 when the former Prince of Wales, now Edward VII, returned to the Medway Towns, Gillingham, or that part of Gillingham once known as New Brompton, was no longer a building site and was viewed as a place fit for a king to visit. While not necessarily of great beauty, the recent creation of a borough council did at least ensure

Kingswood Road, built during the 1880s, was one of many streets in the area of Gillingham once known as New Brompton to fulfil the needs of those employed in the Gillingham extension of the dockyard.

that housing developments were brought under control and that greater attention was given to the overall appearance of the new town through the proper clearance of rubbish, the introduction of a much-needed system of sewage disposal and the laying down of proper footpaths. The dockyard extension was also now complete, and Gillingham was a central element in the massively important military-industrial complex that was the Medway Towns – Gillingham's specialisation was that of repairing and fitting out of the fleet. While ships, and soon submarines, were built at the Chatham end of the dockyard, once launched they were brought to the Gillingham end for the complexities of loading on to them their furnishings, machinery and armament. For this purpose, workshops and stores abounded, with the bulk of the workforce now passing into the dockyard through either Pembroke or Gillingham gates, with Main Gate in Chatham no longer the foremost point of entry into the yard.

As for the reason Edward VII came to Medway in 1905, this was to recognise Gillingham's considerable contribution to the nation's defence. The king was here to both unveil the Royal Engineer's South Africa War memorial in Brompton Barracks and open a new and extensive Royal Naval Hospital on Windmill Hill.

Kingswood Terrace, a group of houses in Kingswood Road, proudly proclaims its year of completion.

Another group of houses competed to meet the needs of those employed on the dockyard, Nelson Road. In this photograph taken at around the time Edward VII visited the town, St Barnabas Chapel, consecrated on 11 June (St Barnabas Day) 1890, helps confirm the date of many of the other properties in this road.

Arriving this time at Rochester railway station, he was first taken along Rochester High Street before entering Dock Road where he paid a brief visit to the Royal Marine Barracks, and then, in the uniform of a field marshal, making the short journey to Brompton Barracks. Here, with his carriage brought to a standstill beside the already existing Crimean War memorial, he was received by the orderly ranks of the 1,500 troops of the depot battalions as he crossed the parade ground where the new memorial was veiled from public view. An occasion organised by the Royal Engineers, it was no simple matter of pulling on an ornate rope or cutting a ribbon – only the latest gadgetry would do. On this occasion, the king was brought to a table where, after a short speech, he pressed a button and electricity did the rest, the veil over the memorial immediately falling away. After all, the Engineers needed to prove their worth, the new electrical school alongside the barracks, then still under construction, was a costly project that eventually amounted to £40,000 (£4.6 million in today's money).

The afternoon was reserved for the Royal Naval Hospital. Changing into the uniform of an admiral, his carriage now drew him through the ostentatiously decorated streets where virtually every house, at the request of the mayor, was bedecked in flags and banners. According to that week's *Rochester, Chatham and Gillingham News*, 'Private residents as well as tradespeople seemed to vie with each other in producing the most pleasing effect in the way of adorning their premises, and it was quite the exception to find a house or shop that had not some embellishment.'

In this rare photograph taken at the time, Edward VII has just completed the unveiling of the South Africa War Memorial Arch at Brompton Barracks. To witness the ceremony, those with invitations were seated in reserved stands (not in view). On the king touching an electric switch, there was a loud crack and the covering over the memorial fell to the ground.

The South African War Memorial seen shortly after its unveiling by Edward VII. The cannon seen is one captured in the Transvaal, while the figure of a crouching Boer rifleman had been lent to the Royal Engineers by Lord Kitchener.

R.E. Barracks and Band, Chatham

A more colourful view of the parade ground of Brompton Barracks and seen here in the decade that preceded the outbreak of the First World War. At the far end of the parade ground is the Crimean War memorial.

Royal Engineers Electrical School, S.M.E, Chatham.

The Royal Engineers Electrical School seen here shortly after its completion in 1907. Designed by Major E. C. S. Moore of the Royal Engineers, it provides a further example of how the Royal Engineers were abreast of new developments and integrating these into their training programmes to ensure the British Army was among the most advanced in the world.

The former Royal Engineers Electrical School, which now serves as the Museum of the Royal Engineers.

The borough council, not to be outdone, had turned street lighting into elaborate schemes in which shields were displayed on a background of coloured bunting. Every street on his route to the hospital was crowded with well-wishers and, as he passed the junction of the High Street with Canterbury Street, some 600 children grouped in the spacious grounds of St Mark's Church sang the national anthem with 'capital effect'. Eventually the king arrived at the hospital where, according to the *Chatham Observer*,

> The scene was brilliant in the extreme. The entire space in front of the Administration Block was a mass of light uniforms and gay dresses, while the pavilion around about it was crowded with officers. The three Mayors [those of Chatham, Gillingham and Rochester], in their robes and preceded by their mace bearers, took up their positions in the centre of the grandstand, being accompanied by the town clerks of Chatham, Gillingham and the Recorder of Rochester. The aldermen and councillors of Gillingham were placed on the right of the reception pavilion, where a splendid view of the proceedings could be obtained.

To this was added: 'Round after round of cheering could be heard from the streets some minutes before the King arrived, his carriage drawing up punctually at the time appointed, 2.55. A naval guard of honour presented arms, and the Depot Band played the National Anthem.'

The opening ceremony was short and to the point. Following a brief dedication and a psalm that was sung by the choir of the dockyard church, the king was given a gold key for opening the main door of the building, declaring in a loud voice, 'this hospital now open'.

The Royal Naval Hospital, as completed at this time, was a sprawling mass of buildings constructed on a 29-acre site. Very much in the style of the day, each had distinctive facings of red brick and Doulton stone – the latter acquired from Somerset. Designed by J. T. C. Murray, construction work had been supervised by S. P. Brinon, one of the Admiralty's own architects.

Edward VII passing through the streets of Gillingham on his way to open the new naval hospital.

As the king passed St Mark's Church, 600 schoolchildren sang the national anthem.

Within the spacious grounds were, in fact, two separate hospitals administered as one unit. Closest to the hospital was a general entrance, made up of wards and various ancillary buildings. Designed on the pavilion principle, they were all connected by a huge corridor, 1,000 feet in length. Also, and close to the general hospital, was a smaller, isolation or zymotic hospital for those with contagious diseases. Other buildings included an administration block, a chapel and accommodation for the staff. Like the rest of the hospital, they were of red brick, although the chapel had Portland stone dressing.

At the time of its opening, the hospital was considered a tremendous advance, the local papers boasting of electric lighting and steam radiators together with up-to-date operating theatres dispensaries and modern sanitation. The hospital was equipped for over 500 patients, having nine medical officers, one head ward master, seven sisters and around seventy sick berth ratings.

Having opened the hospital, the king was to return to the royal train, which was brought to Gillingham station for him to board and journey back to Victoria. Again, the streets between the hospital and the station were lined with enthusiastic crowds. It was observed by one local reporter that while the cheering was continuous, it was not so demonstrative as would have been given in what some would consider 'less correct towns.' This reporter went on to add that those in Gillingham seemed reluctant to cheer, 'evidently from a notion that it looked somewhat undignified'. An interesting social observation, for most of those lining the streets would have been families of those employed in the dockyard, the male breadwinners invariably highly skilled artisans with a certain standing in the community, and to show unbridled enthusiasm was clearly not the done thing. There was a clear line not to be stepped over, for these were very respectable folk holding very respectable positions.

The king officially opens the Royal Naval Hospital in Gillingham. Following a brief dedication and a psalm that was sung by the choir of the dockyard church, the king was given a specially made golden key for opening the main door of the building. In words clearly heard, he declared 'this hospital now open'.

A view through the entrance gate looking into Gillingham's Royal Naval Hospital. The Gillingham Royal Naval Hospital was to remain in service hands until 1961 when it was acquired by the NHS for civilian use, reopening again in 1965 as Medway Hospital. Since then the hospital has undergone numerous further improvements, including an extension in 1970 that allowed it to become the main accident and emergency centre for north Kent, a further extension in 1990 for elderly and mental health services, and a £60 million development in 1999 that doubled the hospital in size. It was with this 1999 extension that it also gained a new name, Medway Maritime, reflecting the earlier connection with the Royal Naval Hospital. More recently a new £11.5 million Accident and Emergency department has been added to the hospital, which opened in November 2018.

It was at 4.05 p.m. precisely that the royal train rolled up and the king took his seat in a handsomely furnished carriage. Giving a parting bow, he left amid renewed demonstrations of loyalty from thousands of spectators in the vicinity of Victoria Bridge, Kingswood and Balmoral roads. Timed to perfection was a twenty-one-gun salute, fired from Fort Amherst.

DID YOU KNOW?
During the 1950s and resulting from the continued growth of Gillingham and the Medway Towns in general, hospital facilities were fully stretched, leading to a decision to build a new hospital adjacent to the Hoath Way. This hospital would have been built during the 1960s had not an announcement been made in July 1959 that the Royal Naval Hospital, as opened by Edward VII, was now surplus to naval needs and was to be given over to civilian use. It became Medway Hospital, with the then Ministry of Health setting aside £1 million for its modernisation.

8. The Tram Graveyard

On 30 September 1930 a tramway system running across the Medway Towns ceased to operate, replaced by fifty-one double-deck petrol-driven buses. The question immediately arose as what to do with an entire fleet of trams that was now nothing more than an inconvenience. An obvious solution was to sell them, but who would want an old, well-used tram? One suggestion put forward by the owners, the Chatham & District Light Railways Company, was that aspiring house owners might like to buy them, suggesting that they would make excellent one-storey residences, with the open deck easily turned into a roof garden!

DID YOU KNOW?
On being taken out of service at midnight on 30 September 1930, the trams that once served Gillingham were immediately put up for sale – the price a mere £5. Apart from possible use as a bungalow with a roof garden, other suggestions included turning the cars into sports pavilions or summerhouses. There were few takers.

In the meantime, sold or not, approximately seventy trams would need to be stored somewhere. It was not possible to simply take them to the tram depot at Luton as this facility was needed for the brand-new fleet of buses; nor could they be left out in the street laid up on their original trackway as this would block the movement of all other vehicles. Fortunately, a solution was at hand. Each tram was taken to a final resting place in Gillingham and placed, nose to tail, on a trackway that ran alongside Watling Street. In fact, this was the only stretch of tramway throughout the Medway Towns that did not run through a street, this land having been purchased and turned into a tram-only freeway by the Chatham & District Light Railways Company in 1906 when an extension of the system into Rainham had been created, running from Jezreel's corner.

Throughout the period of trams running in Medway, Gillingham had been especially well served. Between the opening of the service in June 1902, trams had run from Borstal, Frindsbury and Strood via Rochester and Chatham into Old Brompton and Gillingham town centre, terminating at either Gillingham Green or Victoria Bridge. In addition, a service also ran into Gillingham by way of Chatham Hill and Watling Street with that service later extended into Rainham.

The Gillingham tram graveyard, the last resting place of the Medway trams prior to being sent off to the breakers' yard.

A further view of the Gillingham graveyard for trams.

The stretch of land alongside Watling Street that had been purchased as a separate trackway for trams and used in 1930 for the laying up of the tramway fleet upon its replacement by petrol-driven buses.

Trams served many parts of Gillingham, with the most frequent services running between Old Brompton and Gillingham Town. This photograph shows two trams about to pass each other in the High Street.

A Chatham and Rochester-bound tram approaching the London and Provincial Bank (now Barclays) in the High Street.

Today it is difficult to believe that Gillingham's pedestrianised High Street was once a busy thoroughfare frequently used by trams and, later, motor buses.

As for the graveyard, this was to continue seeing the storage of the old fleet of trams for several weeks, becoming in itself a visitor attraction, with even postcards of the trams as laid up sold in local shops and other pictures appearing in various newspapers around the country. It was a novel site, but for some tinged with sadness. After all, the trams had been a part of Gillingham life for over a quarter of a century. Eventually, with no takers for their use as bungalows (although six did end up on a farm in Lidsing, lingering there until 1966), the remaining sixty or so passed over to a breakers yard and were scrapped. Nowadays, of course, they would be valued by any museum as a fascinating aspect of transport history.

DID YOU KNOW?
Trams operated across Gillingham and the other Medway Towns for a total of twenty-eight years, with one tram driver, Thomas William Horn, notching up an accident-free record of more than 500,000 miles. Many drivers recorded 200,000 miles of tram driving in the three towns.

Another tram perambulating the High Street, with this one bound for Chatham Cemetery.

9. Too Little, Too Late

The announcement on 3 September 1939 by Prime Minister Neville Chamberlain that 'this country is at war with Germany' could have come as no surprise to anyone living in Gillingham. As each day passed since Hitler had assumed power in January 1933, such a possibility had seemed increasingly likely. An earlier outbreak of war with Germany, in October 1938, had been narrowly avoided by Chamberlain's return from Munich with a worthless piece of paper held high; but it had given the country breathing space, if nothing more. The ten months that followed at least provided an opportunity for the nation to get its act together, with too much time having been wasted ignoring the rise of Nazi Germany. For Gillingham, in common with many towns and cities, the months that preceded the Munich Agreement had seen little done to protect the civilian population from the inevitable. By contrast, the following months saw many towns desperately trying to put in place an effective system of civil defence. Gillingham, however, remained fairly complacent – strange, given that, through the existence of the dockyard, the town and its large civilian population was likely to become a prime target for enemy bombers.

With war finally breaking out in September 1939, past events might well have been reflected upon. Gillingham had been far from unscathed by the First World War, with not a family untouched by the death or injury of a loved one. Particularly horrific was the aerial bombing of the naval barracks exactly twenty-two years earlier – German Gotha bombers had struck on the evening of 3 September 1917. A single bomb dropped on the gymnasium, used as overflow sleeping accommodation, resulted in the death of over 130 naval ratings and seriously injuring a further ninety. No other bomb dropped in

The true meaning of war was frequently witnessed in Gillingham during the First World War, with many locally based ships and crews lost through enemy action. Two such losses occurred in the River Medway: massive explosions on board the battleship *Bulwark* and the mine-layer *Princess Irene*. Both disasters were witnessed from the Gillingham shoreline and memorialised in the naval section of the Woodlands Road Cemetery.

For Gillingham, an even greater tragedy was the death of some 130 naval ratings killed by a single German bomb that fell on the naval barracks on 3 September 1917. This memorial stands in the Woodlands Road Cemetery.

The years after the First World War held bitter memories of what a further war might bring about. The numerous war memorials in Gillingham, such as this one in Brompton, are the focus of an annual Remembrance Day service.

A separate memorial to those who fell in the First World War was placed at the junction of High Street, Mill Road, Brompton Road and Marlborough Road, but later moved to its present location on the fringe of the Black Lion Playing Field (now Medway Park).

Also in Gillingham, while overlooking the town of Chatham, is the Naval War Memorial, first unveiled in 1924. At that time, it memorialised the more than 50,000 men and women who lost their lives while serving with the Royal Navy during the First World War.

that entire war came close to equalling this number of fatalities as inflicted by that one bomb dropped on Gillingham.

As well as recalling that particular tragedy, many would also be aware of a much larger number of naval ratings and officers who had been attached to HMS *Pembroke* and who had died while serving the country at sea. As for those living in the town of Gillingham in early 1918, many families, especially the poorest, had suffered in another way. They had come near to starvation due to severe food shortages. A riot in the High Street was only narrowly avoided when one shop, one of the few in the town with stocks of margarine, refused to sell this essential item for cooking to non-regular customers. Only the direct intervention of the chairman of a recently formed borough Food Control Committee prevented a serious disturbance. On that occasion, he had ordered that the shop supply all in the queue with margarine in ½lb packets. In that same month, due to a shortage of cattle being brought into the nearby market at Rochester, no meat was available for the butchers of Gillingham.

Reinforcing the memory of what had happened during the First World War, especially the immense loss of life, were the war memorials that had been erected across the borough and which included the huge national naval memorial on the Lines. Each served as a poignant and constant reminder as to the folly of war and what was likely to occur in any future war. Such thoughts especially came to mind on each Armistice Day, 11 November, when special services were held alongside each of those memorials and also in each church and chapel of the borough. At 11 a.m. on each Armistice Day, there were few in Gillingham who would not, during the two-minute silence, cease whatever they were doing and reflect upon the terrible toll of injury and death in that far from distant conflict that had gained so little.

The likelihood of another war had been firmly brought home to Gillingham by the Munich Agreement of October 1938, bringing with it the fear that the town would once again be subject to aerial bombardment. Galvanised into action, the borough authorities had ordered the digging of make-shift trenches in public parks and open spaces with these to serve as emergency air-raid shelters. Nothing else was possible for, in common with most other boroughs across the country, Gillingham had no effective plans for civil defence. In that month of October, gas masks were hastily issued, and homeowners advised to create a room secure against a poison-gas attack and reinforced against the effect of explosive bombs. Of course, there were no evacuation plans for schoolchildren and nursing mothers and family air-aid shelters were not even a distant dream.

Fortunately for Gillingham, war did not break out in October 1938, with the town not to see the return of enemy bombers until the summer of 1940. During that time an improved system of civil defence was certainly introduced, with critics stating that more should have been done. Not helping matters was a resistance by the borough council (the body responsible for all civil defence matters) to combining their efforts with those of Rochester and Chatham. In doing so, money could have been more equitably shared and an overall co-ordinated plan achieved. After all, the three towns were relatively small and nestled so closely together as to be indistinguishable from each other. However, when calls were made for these three boroughs to work together, zealous councillors, tied to the concept of the parish pump, quickly overruled such ideas. In February 1938, a scheme mooted to employ just one chief ARP officer to oversee the three boroughs was soundly rejected, leading to each borough creating their own separate departments, with Gillingham appointing Captain R. Travers Griffin as their borough ARP officer. In joining together, the three towns would have been an ideal unit for civil defence planning as all three were part of the same military-industrial complex supporting a large workforce whose homes straddled the area. Irrespective of whether these workers and their families lived in Rochester, Chatham or Gillingham, all had needs that were exactly the same and their chances of getting bombed only differed according to their proximity to the naval dockyard.

It was an overall lack of adequate progress in recruiting volunteers and establishing a full and robust civil defence network to serve the community that resulted in Sir Auckland Geddes, the Commissioner for Civil Defence for the south-east region, to lay it on thick that Gillingham really needed to get its act together. In a meeting attended by members of the borough council held in June 1939 at the Pavilion (then a dance hall at the lower end of Canterbury Street) he bluntly informed his audience that when the war comes, 'you here in Gillingham are in a position at which one of the very earliest blows of all may fall.' For this reason, he declared, it was essential that the shortcomings in civil defence be immediately rectified, going on to list where the town's organisation needed to be immediately improved. Using figures presented to him by the Gillingham ARP department he told of how the town was in desperate need of air-raid wardens, first aid parties, decontamination parties, firemen and motor drivers. In total, the borough had only 428 volunteers, but they needed a further 1,088. Geddes considered this to be an appalling situation for a town that would be 'so exposed' to enemy bombing.

It was not just a shortage of volunteers in which Gillingham was to be found wanting when it came to the actual outbreak of war just two months later. The evacuation of schoolchildren to areas considered safe from bombing was one example. As with many authorities, these plans were hastily cobbled together in August, with a full mock evacuation carried out at the end of that month when only 600 of the borough's 7,985 schoolchildren were available to participate. On that occasion it was deemed a complete success. These children marched from their school to Gillingham railway station to meet thirteen trains, which were timed to arrive at half-hourly intervals. Just four days later, the real evacuation took place. This time a total of 2,493 children were brought either to Gillingham or Rainham stations, but the vast majority of parents simply refused to allow their children to be evacuated. As a result, most trains left half-empty. In many ways, it was hard to blame those parents, given that the information with which they were provided, and upon which they were releasing their children for an unknown period of time, was in a circular sent out from each school that simply stated:

> It will be impossible before the children leave home for the parents to be told where they are going, but arrangements will be made for the parents to be informed by post of their whereabouts within 24 hours. No expense on the part of parents either in respect of transport or maintenance will be involved, and as far as possible, children of the same family will be kept together, whether they attend the same school or not.

In the naval dockyard during the 1920s and early 1930s work had been greatly reduced, with few new ships being launched. A revival in warship building had already taken place by the time of the Munich Agreement, with the submarine *Seal* launched at the yard on 27 September 1938 – war at that time seeming only days away. *Seal* provided work for many dockyard workers living in Gillingham.

Parents were advised:

> Children will be required to take with them an overcoat or raincoat, a blanket and food for one whole day, light luggage including at least one change of underclothing, and stockings, soap, tooth brush and respirator. Children must be ready to assemble as soon as they receive instructions to do so.

As it happens, evacuation trains from Gillingham were to take those children into the countryside of east Kent. In the event, a somewhat poor choice given the turn of events that took place in 1940 when these same children needed to be re-evacuated into Wales to avoid being in the midst of a potential battlefield should the Germans mount a successful invasion.

In only evacuating such a small number, the authorities in Gillingham had to face up to a further problem: what to do with the more than 5,000 schoolchildren remaining in the borough? In assuming that the evacuation would be a total success, with all schoolchildren together with teachers and their wives removed from the borough, all schools had been closed and given over to ARP workers. This also permitted those schools with air-raid shelters, as provided by the county council and not the borough, to be designated as public shelters, so helping make up for an overall lack of shelters as provided by the borough council. Adding to the overall problem was that some of the schools that were closed should have remained open. These were ones in Rainham, a rural area where many families lived in a non-evacuation zone not far from where London children were being sent. As a result, these rural children of Gillingham were totally deprived of any opportunity to even attend a school.

The Municipal Buildings in Canterbury Street served as the headquarters of the borough's civil defence organisation. Chief Warden Travers Griiffin had his headquarters and communication room to the rear of the building. First opened in September 1937, the roof of the building was fitted with one of the borough's several air-raid sirens.

Gillingham railway station as it appeared during the period of evacuation in September 1939.

With the increasing awareness that war with Germany was inevitable, air-raid shelters started to become available in shops, such as Timothy White's in Gillingham High Street, during the early months of 1939.

One of the surface shelters that were later built by Gillingham Borough Council and which, in this case, survived a bomb exploding nearby.

A surviving public air-raid shelter in Brompton, located in a field just off Maxwell Road.

Although Gillingham was the target for a number of air raids during the Second World War, the town got off relatively lightly when compared with the devastation wreaked upon two other major naval dockyards towns – those of Plymouth and Portsmouth. For Gillingham, one particularly serious raid was late on 27 August 1940 when bombs fell throughout Gillingham with many casualties and destruction, as seen in this photograph of the bus station in Nelson Road. (Courtesy of the M&D and East Kent Bus Club)

The provision of public shelters was a further area in which there was a clear failure on the part of Gillingham's ARP provision, with no purpose-built shelters constructed by the borough prior to the outbreak of war. This was despite the county council building shelters in schools for children attending those schools, the Admiralty building shelters for those in the dockyard and naval barracks and Short Brothers in Rochester digging a deep shelter into the chalk cliffs behind the seaplane works on the Esplanade. Other councils in Kent, equally as vulnerable as Gillingham, namely Dover and Ramsgate, had also built deep shelters to secure the entire population of those respective towns from air raids.

By October 1939 Gillingham Town Council was proudly boasting that it had a total of sixteen public shelters available, but in looking more closely at those shelters, a quarter of them had been built by the county council for the now closed schools, while others had been formed out of road subways, open trenches built in parks, a converted public convenience and even a park entrance. Those make-shift conversions had been created through the simple process of sandbagging the walls and providing a protecting screen to the entrance. Fortunately, by that time a hasty programme was also underway, with several shelters to be constructed, but these mostly above ground and in no way capable of withstanding either a direct hit or a nearby blast.

DID YOU KNOW?

Coinciding with the announcement that the nation was at war, movie fans in Gillingham suffered a particular blow. It was announced that all cinemas were to close for fear of a high death rate in the event of a bombing raid. Two weeks later this order was rescinded as it was realised that films were important to the nation's morale. Films that should have been screened during the first week of war were now screened two weeks later. In reopening, the cinemas of Gillingham, of which there were then three, had to produce clear plans for an effective evacuation procedure, with the *Embassy* in Green Street, upon the sounding of an air-raid alarm, immediately placing on the screen a map showing the nearest public shelter. Unfortunately, that shelter could accommodate little more than fifty, while the Embassy, more recently a sports bar and activities centre, had an audience capacity of more than 1,700.

The one-time Embassy cinema on Green Street.

About the Author

Philip MacDougall has been researching and writing about the history of Gillingham and the Medway Towns for a number of years, with his first book, *The Story of the Hoo Peninsula*, published in 1980. In all, he has written nearly twenty books on the area, including *The Book of Medway* (published in 1989), *Chatham Dockyard: The Rise and Fall of a Military Industrial Complex* (2012), *Medway Towns at Work* (2017) and two companion volumes to this present title, *Secret Chatham* (2016) and *Secret Rochester* (2019). As well as writing about the Medway area, Philip has a recognised expertise in naval history, writing in depth on the supporting infrastructure of various navies across the world, concentrating especially on the eighteenth century. Philip has also contributed biographical material on selected naval officers for the widely acclaimed *Dictionary of National Biography*. In addition, he has family connections with the navy of the eighteenth century, an ancestor having served as Nelson's personal secretary during the naval wars fought against France, having first joined that future great admiral at the Nore anchorage off the Isle of Grain in 1793.